WEAPON

THE MOSIN-NAGANT RIFLE

BILL HARRIMAN

Series Editor Martin Pegler

First published in Great Britain in 2016 by Osprey Publishing,
PO Box 883, Oxford, OX1 9PL, UK
1385 Broadway, 5th Floor, New York, NY 10018, USA
E-mail: info@ospreypublishing.com

Osprey Publishing, part of Bloomsbury Publishing Plc

A CIP catalogue record for this book is available from the British
Library

Print ISBN: 978 1 4728 1415 9
PDF ebook ISBN: 978 1 4728 1416 6
ePub ebook ISBN: 978 1 4728 1417 3

Index by Rob Munro
Typeset in Sabon and Univers
Originated by PDQ Media, Bungay, UK
Printed in China through World Print Ltd.

16 17 18 19 20   10 9 8 7 6 5 4 3 2 1

Osprey Publishing supports the Woodland Trust, the UK's leading
woodland conservation charity. Between 2014 and 2018 our
donations are being spent on their Centenary Woods project in
the UK.

www.ospreypublishing.com

Front cover, above: A Mosin-Nagant M1891 Dragoon rifle.
(Armémuseum/The Swedish Army Museum)
Front cover, below: Russian infantrymen of World War I armed
with Mosin-Nagant rifles. (Public Domain)
Title page: A Soviet cavalryman has trained his horse to lie down
to provide cover for him. He lies behind the animal's body and
rests his M1891/30 rifle on the saddle in a firing position. This
practice was common in many armies, affording the soldier very
good protection from enemy fire. Although seemingly a heartless
act, training a horse to lie down did at least minimize the chances
of the animal being hit, as it offered a smaller target prone than
when standing. (Nik Cornish at www.stavka.org.uk)

Dedication

To my wife, Janet and my daughters, Annabel and Caroline; with
thanks for their forbearance about my obsession with old
firearms.

Acknowledgements

I would like to thank Jon Ferguson and Mark Murray-Flutter of
the Royal Armouries Museum, Leeds; my *Antiques Roadshow*
colleague, Martin Pegler; and my editor, Nick Reynolds at Osprey
for his support, guidance and tolerance.

Editor's note

In this book, the Julian calendar is used for events prior to 1917;
the Gregorian calendar is used for events after that year. Metric
units of measurement have been employed, with the exception of
calibres. For pre-1924 Russian measurements, the original
measurements are given, accompanied by a conversion into
metric. The line was an archaic Russian measurement equal to
.100 of an English inch. The *arshin* or cubit was a Russian
measurement equal to 28 English inches or 71.12cm. This system
of measurement was abolished in 1924 when the Soviet Union
adopted the metric system.

CONTENTS

INTRODUCTION

For the last 40 years I have collected infantry rifles, their bayonets, ammunition and related accessories. Infantry are the most important troops on any battlefield as only they can take and hold ground; and the way a nation arms its infantry says a lot about its tactical doctrine and the way it wages war.

During the 1980s, I worked in Birmingham, UK, for a firm of specialist auctioneers which sold not only militaria but guns – from tiny watch-chain pistol curios to field artillery. It was a fantastic opportunity to learn as well as adding to my already expanding collection. During my time in Birmingham I sold hundreds of Mosin-Nagants – of all types. I used to do some cataloguing work for a firm in Nottingham which had ex-Chinese M1891/30s piled as high as I was, just like cordwood. Yet for all my regular exposure to Mosin-Nagants, I gave them no further thought, often

A Finnish soldier on skis and wearing a snow suit. He has tucked his ski-poles under his arms while holding his rifle at the ready. The rifle's front-sight protector 'ears' are readily discernible, indicating that this is one of the shorter Finnish reworks which appeared between 1924 and 1939. The Finns reduced the M1891's length and added new furniture and sights as part of a modification programme that was far more extensive than that implemented by the Russians in 1930. The Finns used the Mosin-Nagant as the basis for an improved, modern rifle while the Russians only tinkered at the edges of the design. (Photo by Carl Mydans/The LIFE Picture Collection/Getty Images)

referring to them as 'those heaps of Soviet rubbish'. Owing to my stupidity and prejudice I did not see those rifles and carbines for the valuable historical artefacts that they undoubtedly were. To me they were badly made, primitive guns, unworthy of further study or consideration.

It was not until a few years ago, when I took stock of my collection, that I discovered a serious deficiency: there was no representative Mosin-Nagant action in it. I immediately bought one from a dealer friend's website. When it arrived, I was faintly disappointed. It was crude, ill-balanced and appeared to have been restocked. It was only when I bothered to look at it in detail that the scales of ignorance fell from my eyes. What I had was not some crude Soviet mishmash but a Remington-made M1891 rifle captured from the Bolsheviks by the Finns in the 1920s and taken into Finnish service. A rare prize indeed and like most military

ВСТУПАЙТЕ В РЯДЫ НАРОДНОГО ОПОЛЧЕНИЯ!

'Join the rows of the People's Militia Army!' During the Great Patriotic War (1941–45), the Soviet Union issued large numbers of propaganda posters which vilified the Germans (always referred to as 'fascists' by the Soviets) and exhorted workers, peasants and soldiers to struggle for the liberty of the Russian Motherland. The Mosin-Nagant M1891/30 rifle and its bayonet are easily recognizable in many of the posters. This monochrome drawing depicts grim-faced and resolute Soviet soldiers marching with plainly discernible M1891/30 rifles, wearing *pilotka* caps and with their greatcoats *en banderole*. Found in the collection of the Russian State Library, Moscow. (Photo by Fine Art Images/ Heritage Images/Getty Images)

firearms, an open book just waiting to be read. All I needed now was to master its language.

My new acquisition bore the 'SA' Finnish Army property mark and its rear sight had been re-graduated from *arshins* to metres. That in itself was fascinating. It was indeed restocked, but officially so by the Finns. The stock was made in two pieces with finger splices to resist warping in the extreme cold. It bore the mark of an unknown government stocker. When I finally bothered to learn about my Mosin-Nagant, my love affair with the rifle was born and I resolved to find out all I could about it – hence this book.

I found that any amount of Mosin-Nagant accessories – oil bottles, cleaning kits, chargers and ammunition pouches – could be had for pocket-money prices, mainly from internet auction sites. At the time of writing, my collection of oil bottles exceeds 20 different versions. Ammunition is plentiful, too: a 440-round 'sardine' can of ex-Soviet cartridges is cheaper than its equivalent in shotgun shells. Shooting the Mosin-Nagant became a great pleasure and a great eye-opener. Other than excessive muzzle flash from the carbines, it is a pleasant and reliable rifle to shoot.

I hope you enjoy reading this book as much as I have enjoyed writing it. For me, Mosin-Nagant ownership and research has been a voyage of discovery. I hope that you will be inspired to own a piece of history. Perhaps you will have a Mosin-Nagant that marched with the Tsar's army or that defended the Soviet Motherland during the Great Patriotic War. Perhaps your Mosin-Nagant was made in the United States for the Russian war effort in World War I, or perhaps it is a version used to shoot at American soldiers in Vietnam during the 1960s. Whatever it may be, I wish you joy of it. I hope that this book both informs and educates you.

DEVELOPMENT
Towards Russia's new rifle

ORIGINS

On 24 April 1877, Imperial Russia went to war against Ottoman Turkey, principally as a gesture of pan-Slavic solidarity over the wholesale mistreatment of the Christian population of Bulgaria after an abortive rebellion against Ottoman rule. At this time Tsar Alexander II's foot-soldiers were armed with a motley raft of breech-loading rifles, none of which were of Russian design. The majority of the infantry were armed with the '6-line' (15.24×40mmR) Krnka-converted M1856 rifle-musket, but some still carried the '6-line' Carle needle-fire rifle; the Guards, rifle regiments and a few line-infantry regiments were armed with the excellent '4.2-line' (10.75×57.5mmR) M1871 Berdan II bolt-action rifle. The bayonet, rather than aimed rifle fire, was still believed to be the principal weapon for the Russian infantry, as one observer noted:

> They were trained to advance to the attack in column of companies, and to move to the assault while still at a distance from the position to be captured. The bayonet assault was looked upon as the one decisive feature in an infantry attack; no attempt was made to obtain superiority of fire over the enemy. In short the possibilities of the breechloading rifle were not understood. There was no provision for a mobile battalion ammunition reserve which could follow the infantry in the attack. (Quoted in Barry 2012: 80)

Even those Russian soldiers armed with the Berdan II failed to make the most of their modern rifles:

> The rattle of Berdan fire was incessant, but no more prevalent than the replies of the Sniders and Martini-Peabodys from our side. On both

THE MOSIN-NAGANT'S PRECURSORS

In order fully to understand the developmental process that resulted in the Mosin-Nagant M1891 rifle, it is important to understand the design and technology of the three main types of rifle that immediately preceded it.

The Carle rifle

Russia´s first system for converting M1856 rifle-muskets was the Carle needle-fire system, which won a public competition. Johannes Friedrich Christian Carle was a German gunsmith from Suhl who had already invented a breech-loading rifle for paper cartridges. After a few minor alterations the Carle design was adopted on 28 March 1867. To convert a rifle-musket, the lock was removed and the resulting cavity filled in with a wooden plate. The rear of the barrel was cut off and replaced by a breech unit containing a bolt with a leather washer on its tapered head, a long needle, two locking lugs on its body and a coarsely chequered operating knob.

While the Carle system was designed to convert existing muzzle-loaders, new-build examples have been noted – probably purpose built to use up existing components in arsenals – although this weapon is very seldom seen in the West. It was planned to convert 785,295 M1856 rifle-muskets using the Carle system; but by 1874, when the Berdan II began to be produced in quantity, only 215,000 had been converted – and no more were converted after this date. The Carle needle-fire rifles were widely issued to troops of the Caucasus, Turkmenistan, Siberian and Orenburg army districts.

The Carle's cartridge was very similar to that of the 11mm M1866 Chassepot breech-loader and was designed by Colonel Weltischchew, Chairman of the Sestroryetsk Arms Commission. No extant specimen of this cartridge is known; it was combustible and very little residue was left on firing. The cartridge was placed into the loading cut-out and the bolt was pushed forward to chamber the cartridge. The lever was turned to the right to allow the lugs to engage with two slots to lock the action. The bolt handle was pushed forward to cock the needle. When the trigger was pulled, the needle ran forward and punctured the rear of the paper cartridge, hitting a capsule of fulminating mercury and firing the rifle. The leather washer expanded to seal the breech. Rate of fire was about ten shots a minute. As was the case with other needle-gun cartridges, the ammunition was very fragile and especially prone to damage in wet weather. The Carle also suffered from gas leakage from the breech and excessive residue from sustained firing.

The Krnka rifle

By Imperial Decree of 18 March 1869, Tsar Alexander II authorized the conversion of muzzle-loaders by means of the Krnka system. Silvestr Krnka (1825–1903) was a Bohemian gun designer whose hinged breech mechanism was used to convert muzzle-loaders into breech-loaders in much the same way that American inventor and engineer Jacob Snider's breech system was used to convert British Enfield rifles from 1867 onwards.

The stock of the M1856 rifle-musket was made from Arctic birch, finished with a reddish lacquer. The forend cap, trigger guard and buttplate were brass, the buttplate being marked with arsenal marks and a large Romanov eagle on the tang. The screw-retained bands were iron, as was the trigger guard tang which incorporated a small finger spur. The ram rod was also iron with a pierced cup-shaped end. The ram rod was retained on the conversion as a cleaning aid and also as a clearing rod in the event of a stuck case.

The conversions were carried out in Russia´s main arsenal at Tula; gunmakers of the Birmingham Small Arms Trade Association also built Krnka rifles from scratch for the Russians in 1870. The conversion was very simple. The barrel breech was cut off and a brass 'shoe' incorporating a loading 'trough' was screwed onto the rear. (Brass was used because it was cheap to cast and easy to work. Pressures were not excessive, hence steel or malleable iron was not necessary to contain them.) The shoe incorporated a hinged steel breech-block which swung to the left to expose the chamber. It also carried a striker with a large tapered head which had a flat milled in it to allow the flattened side bar of the replacement hammer to engage it. The hammer did not have a nose. Instead, its percussive effect was communicated to the striker by means of a projection on the left-hand side. The conventional musket hammer was discarded in favour of this projection.

As the block swung full over to the left, it activated a small extractor which started primary extraction of the spent case. The case was only completely removed by raising the rifle to the vertical and allowing it to fall out. This was not really a satisfactory extraction system. In fact, most types of converted breech-loaders concentrated on getting the cartridge *into* the chamber; extraction was very much a secondary consideration.

The whole of the M1856 rifle was badly balanced because of the weight of the brass shoe. The Krnka conversion did nothing to improve the existing failings of the M1856; but on the positive side it was a classic, robustly Russian 'soldier-proof' rifle, ideal for the unsophisticated and largely illiterate soldiers of the Imperial Russian Army. However, bearing in mind that the Russian military were not overly concerned with individual marksmanship and relied

ABOVE A '6-line' Carle M1856/67 needle-fire rifle. The Carle system was originally conceived as a method of converting M1856 rifle-muskets, but some Carle rifles were purpose built, as was the case with this specimen. Note the large, coarsely chequered bolt handle that not only unlocks the bolt for loading but also cocks the needle when it is pulled back into the locked position. (Author's Collection)

ABOVE A '6-line' Russian M1856/69 rifle, converted from an M1856 rifle-musket made in 1864. (Author's Collection)

instead on massed 'human wave' bayonet charges, this potential for inaccuracy did not particularly concern the Tsar's commanders.

By January 1877, Russia had converted over 613,000 rifle-muskets to Krnka breech-loaders, and these weapons armed some 27 divisions in the Russo-Turkish War (1877–78). The M1869 conversion fired a .608-diameter pointed bullet from a 1.58in (40.13mm) case, propelled by 78 grains (5.05g) of powder. The cartridge was roughly 51mm long. The Krnka breech-loader was capable of about ten shots a minute – much better than the muzzle-loader. The Krnka's sight is interesting. A quadrant type retained by a small thumbscrew, it was normally graduated to 600 *arshins*, but some examples – allegedly for sharpshooters – were graduated to 1,200 *arshins*.

Although the conversion was applied to large numbers of muzzle-loaders, the Krnka is rarely seen in the West or anywhere else for that matter. It was notably outclassed by the 11.43×59mmR Peabody-Martini rifles carried by the Turks, and was a second-rate arm when compared with the small numbers of Berdan II rifles that were just starting to be issued to some Russian units.

The Berdan II rifle

Having bought Russia some breathing-space by instituting two systems for converting its obsolete M1856 rifle-muskets from muzzle-loaders to breech-loaders, the Tsar's military leaders now applied themselves to finding a suitable, purpose-built breech-loading rifle. In the late 1860s, Europe was awash with many excellent designs – the Mauser, Peabody-Martini, Albini and Mannlicher, to name but four. Governments could pick and choose, so there was a good choice to be had as inventor vied with inventor to secure the Holy Grail of gun-making: a government contract.

Colonel Hiram Berdan (1824–93) had commanded the famous 1st and 2nd US Volunteer Sharpshooter regiments during the American Civil War (1861–65). As well as being a soldier, Berdan was a prolific inventor, an excellent marksman and a very competent engineer. He is remembered today for the invention of the Berdan primer, which continues to be used in military cartridges. (Most civilian cartridges use the primer invented in the United Kingdom by his contemporary, Colonel Edward Mounier Boxer RA (1822–98).) After considering several different actions, the Russians chose Berdan's trapdoor action, heavily modified (by mutual agreement) by General Alexander Gorloff, the Russian military attaché in Washington, DC. Some 30,000 of what has become known as the Berdan I rifle were procured from Colt's in the United States. This rifle fired a 10.6mm cartridge, developed by Berdan in cooperation with Gorloff and a Captain K.U. Gunius. The cartridge had a flat trajectory and was quite powerful, generating some 2,340 joules of kinetic energy.

The model adopted in large quantities in 1870 by Russia was a bolt-action design made by Berdan. The design was granted US Patent No. 108,869 of 1 November 1870, but Berdan subsequently sold the patent to the Russian Government. Simple, accurate and reliable, the Berdan II (as it has been designated by arms historians) compared well to European and American rifles of the 1870s. The bolt was very simple and comprised only six components. It had no locking lugs; instead it relied upon the shoulder which carried the small pear-shaped operating knob which locked off against the right side of the split receiver. The knob remained in the 2 o'clock position when closed. A long-range sight for massed volley fire was added after 1879. After the adoption of the 7.62×54mmR cartridge, 200,000 Berdan IIs were altered to use the cartridge by lining their barrels and fitting new bolts with locking lugs on their heads, this being necessary to cope with the increased pressures from the 7.62×54mmR cartridge.

Early Berdan IIs were made in the UK by Birmingham Small Arms using machinery made by Greenwood & Batley of Leeds, who also supplied machinery to Russia for use in its state arsenals. Some 3,500,000 Berdan IIs were made up to 1891 by the Tula, Izhevsk and Sestroryetsk arsenals. The Berdan II made a good showing in the Russo-Turkish War, although it was only available to some Russian units. It was also issued to many troops during the Russo-Japanese War (1904–05) and even survived into World War I in the hands of reserve troops.

ABOVE A '4.2-line' M1870 Berdan II bolt-action rifle made by the Tula Arsenal. The sling loops on this example are non-standard; they were normally attached to the top barrel band and the front of the trigger guard. (NRA Museums, NRAMuseums.com)

This painting by Vasili Vasilyevich Vereshchagin (1842–1904) depicts an incident during the capture of Khiva (then in Turkmenistan, now in Uzbekistan) by Russian forces in the early 1870s. Although this is a painting, the detail is almost photographically good and enables confirmation that the rifles depicted are M1856/67 Krnka conversions. Imperial Russia mounted many punitive expeditions against Turkmenistan as part of what it saw as a European crusade against 'Asian barbarity'. (Fine Art Images)

sides there was an enormous waste of cartridges, aim being taken, where it was taken at all, at impracticable distances; but more frequently the great object of the men was to engage in a rapid firing competition, and get rid of as many shots as possible in a given space of time. (Quoted in Barry 2012: 182)

An NCO in the Vladimir Regiment who was about 1,800m away from the Turks during the fight for Plevna in 1877 lamented that although he could see Russian soldiers taking casualties from Turkish Peabody-Martini rifles at that range, the inadequacy of the Krnka rifle made return fire impossible:

We had not been long in the vineyard when the Turks began to fire at us. Many of our men were wounded before the order was given to advance ... and among them the Captain of my company who was lying down among the vines ... Men fell on all sides, in the front ranks and rear sections alike ... When at last we moved forward, the bullets fell upon us like hail ... We had not gone more than 50 paces when the officer of my sub-division was struck in the chest. We could not fire. Our Krnka rifles were only sighted up to 600 yards [550m] and the Turks were a verst and one half [1,600m] away. Long before we got near the [Turkish] trenches there was no one left to advance. (Quoted in Bradley 1990: 127)

When the Russo-Turkish War was concluded by the Treaty of San Stefano of 3 March 1878, the Russians took stock of the whole affair. They had suffered appalling casualties at the hands of dug-in Turkish troops at Plevna armed with advanced US-made breech-loaders such as Peabody-Martinis and Winchester Model 1866 repeaters. The Russians' rag-tag selection of breech-loaders was clearly not up to the mark and they needed to rearm.

During the last two decades of the 19th century, firearms technology was changing rapidly. The new desideratum for an infantry rifle was that it had to be of smaller calibre (6–8mm), use the newly developed smokeless propellants and be a magazine repeater. The French effectively set the standard when, in 1886, they adopted the 8mm Lebel M1886 rifle. Germany followed in 1888 with a hastily designed Mauser/Mannlicher/Mieg hybrid and the Swiss followed suit soon after. The architect of Russian rearmament in the late 1860s, Dmitri Alekseyevich Miliutin (1816–1912) – Minister of War (1861–81) under Tsar Alexander II – said during the early 1880s: 'Since 1866 we have changed the entire weaponry of our infantry ... first from smoothbore muskets ... to rifles then to rapid fire arms. In 1860 we had but 216,000 muskets ... in our arsenals. At the present time we have more than 1 million rapid fire rifles' (quoted in Bradley 1990: 117). Miliutin's satisfaction did not last long, however, for developments in firearms technology moved at such great speed in the 1870s and 1880s that rearmament was short-lived, and the whole process had to be gone through yet again by the beginning of the 1890s.

Despite the appalling casualties sustained by the Imperial Russian Army in the Russo-Turkish War, it still took five years for the bureaucratic Russian military even to begin to do something about finding a new rifle. In 1883, Russia's Central Artillery Directorate convened a commission under Major-General N.I. Chagin to study and test magazine repeating rifles with a view to replacing the Berdan II. After 1886, the Chagin Commission's focus turned to small-bore repeaters using smokeless powders since the advent of the Lebel rifle. Not everyone in Russian military circles was persuaded that a new rifle was needed, however. A contemporary survey of military rifles in 1889 by a Captain Franz Holzner, which was subsequently translated and presented to the Royal Artillery Institution by Major W. McClintock RA, noted that 'In the Russian Army Lieut-Generals Cebiseff and Dragomiroff object to a reduction in the size of bore' (McClintock 1889: 32).

Russian soldiers take cover in an earthwork from enemy fire during the Russo-Turkish War (1877–78). Senior officers observe from the left-hand side. The artist has depicted the rifles with brass forend caps, meaning that they are M1856 rifle-muskets converted to breech-loading by either the Carle or the Krnka systems. This anonymous work dating from 1877–78 is in the collections of Moscow's Tretyakov Gallery. (Photo by: Photo12/UIG via Getty Images)

TOWARDS THE MOSIN-NAGANT

One of the Commission's members, Captain Sergei Ivanovich Mosin (1849–1902), had already designed a magazine for the Berdan rifle. Mosin had enrolled in a military school in 1861 and had joined the Alexandrovskoye Military High School in Moscow by 1867. He then went to the Mikhailovskoye Artillery School in St Petersburg in 1870 where he was commissioned lieutenant in 1872. From there he transferred to the Tula Arsenal and became tool-room supervisor in about 1878.

Mosin submitted a '3-line' (7.62mm) rifle to the arms trials. A Belgian gun designer, Émile Nagant (1830–1902), submitted a '3.5-line' (9mm) rifle. The Commission favoured Nagant's offering even though it had a complicated dismantling process that needed special tools – hardly a positive recommendation for military use. Mosin's rifle also suffered from problems with materials and was not reliable. The Commission duly voted for the Nagant, 14 votes to 10. Major-General Chagin, in his capacity as President of the Commission, ordered further tests, however, and the Commission finally settled on a hybrid version of the two rifles after witnessing an improved performance by the Mosin.

The Nagant features of the hybrid rifle were the cartridge interrupter under the bolt which prevented double loading, and the distinctive magazine follower. Nagant had opted for a single-stack, five-round magazine with an 'N'-shaped follower and spring that could be detached from the magazine body simply by squeezing the cartridge platform against the floor-plate and removing it from a pivot in the front of the magazine. The floor-plate could be unlatched using the thumb alone to allow the magazine to be unloaded. The magazine – it was not unlike that of the Belgian 7.65mm Mauser Model 1889 bolt-action rifle, and may indeed have been influenced by it – was loaded by means of a five-round spring steel charger. The bolt cocked on closing and had two locking lugs on the detachable head. Unlike other rifle designs, however, the lugs were unlocked when they were in the 12 and 6 o'clock positions in the action. When the bolt was locked, the lugs assumed the 9 and 3 o'clock positions. The bolt was made in two pieces linked by a connector bar. (The resemblance to the French Lebel M1886 bolt cannot go unremarked. This is unsurprising given the close degree of *détente* between France and Russia at that time, with the Franco-Russian Alliance treaty being in the advanced stages of negotiation prior to its finalization in early 1894.) The rear sight was graduated to 2,700 *arshins*.

From December 1890 onwards, the hybrid rifle underwent extensive troop trials with the Life-Guards Izmailovskii Regiment, Life-Guards Pavlovskii Regiment and 147th (Samara) Infantry Regiment at the Infantry Officers' School at Oranienbaum. In January 1891, Nagant patented the interrupter even though he had got the idea for it from Mosin. After some cooperation between Mosin and Nagant, Russia finally adopted the hybrid rifle – called the 'Trehlinejnaja Vintovka Mosina Obrasca 1891 Goda' ('Three Line Rifle Model of the Year 1891') – by decree of Tsar Alexander III on 16 April 1891.

Even though his design had not been accepted, Émile Nagant alleged patent infringement and threatened to withdraw from any further

THE MOSIN-NAGANT EXPOSED

7.62×54mmR M1891 Mosin-Nagant rifle

1. Front sight
2. Barrel
3. Barrel bands
4. Front sling loop slot
5. Handguard
6. Rear sight
7. Rear sling loop slot
8. Buttplate
9. Buttstock

10. Sling
11. Cleaning rod
12. Barrel band
13. Bayonet
14. Locking ring
15. Bayonet socket
16. Cartridge in chamber
17. Firing pin
18. Firing-pin spring

19. Bolt
20. Cocking piece/safety
21. Trigger
22. Trigger guard
23. Cartridges in magazine
24. Magazine follower and spring
25. Magazine floorplate

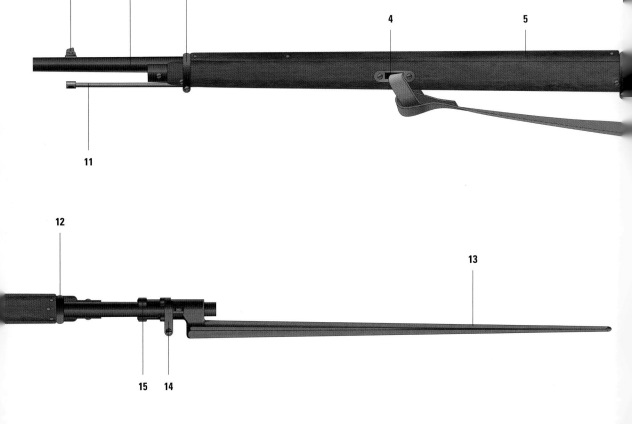

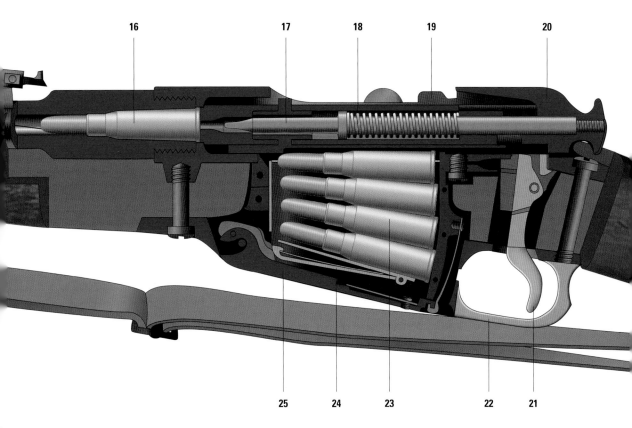

16   17   18   19   20

25   24   23   22   21

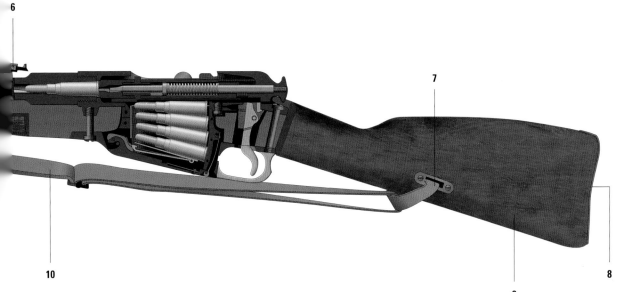

6

7

10

9

8

THIS PAGE Three views of a 7.62×54mmR M1891 rifle, made in 1911 at the Sestroryetsk Arsenal. The breech bears the Romanov eagle cipher of Tsar Nicholas II. The slot has the slots for the strapped sling. Earlier versions had conventional loops and a small finger spur on the trigger guard. (NRA Museums, NRA Museums.com)

OPPOSITE Russian soldiers patrolling a Siberian forest during the Russo-Japanese War (1904–05). This is a very idealized magazine image painted in monochrome from a photograph. The soldiers wear the *bashlyk* cowl over their caps for warmth, with its ends neatly crossing the chest and tucked into the waist belt. The rifle is supposed to depict the M1891 but the bayonet protrudes from under the barrel rather than its right-hand side. The officer on the extreme left is identifiable by his pistol lanyard and slung sword. (Photo by: SeM/ UIG via Getty Images)

Russian arms trials. (Sergei Mosin could not benefit from any patent design features as being an Imperial Russian Army officer, he was deemed to be a state employee. He was made the director of the Sestroryetsk Arsenal in 1894 and eventually became a major-general; he died in 1902 and is buried in Sestroryetsk.) For their part, the Russians threatened to ban Nagant from participating in further arms trials. The Commission, having an eye to the future in that Nagant was generally cooperative and prepared to share Western technology, awarded him 200,000 roubles (the premium paid to Mosin) for his efforts. This policy of conciliation paid dividends as Russia would adopt Nagant's 7.62mm gas-seal revolver design in 1895. (For all that, the joint-name Mosin-Nagant is a Western invention; only the Mosin part was used in Russia.)

Improving the M1891

In 1893 the Mosin-Nagant M1891 rifle underwent minor modifications including the removal of the spur finger rest from the trigger-guard tang and the replacement of ordinary sling-swivels with reinforced slots in the stock for the leather straps of the distinctive Russian sling that was used on all Mosin-Nagants until production ended in the 1950s.

In 1908 a lighter 'spitzer'-type bullet was adopted, necessitating a change of rear sight to take account of the differing trajectory. The flat leaf sight was changed to what was known as the Konovalov sight (named after its designer), which featured a curved leaf graduated to 3,200 *arshins*. In the years leading up to World War I, the M1891 rifle underwent various minor changes including the addition of a hand guard and stock bolt as well as different types of barrel bands.

Two views of a Russian 7.62×54mmR M1891 Dragoon rifle, with the bolt open. With its shorter barrel, simpler rear sight and spring-retained bands, the Dragoon rifle was to become the basis for the M1891/30 rifle. (Armémuseum/The Swedish Army Museum)

Early Mosin-Nagant variants

Although a slow starter, the M1891 rifle would serve Imperial Russia and then the Soviet Union as their main infantry arm until the adoption of the 7.62mm Simonov SKS-45 self-loading rifle in the 1940s. In addition to the standard infantry rifle with its 77.5cm barrel, a Dragoon rifle with a 73cm barrel and variant rear sight was produced. There was also a rifle for the Cossacks which was identical to the Dragoon rifle, but which would not take a bayonet.

In 1907, a carbine version was issued. Based on the designs of other European carbines, the M1907 had a 51cm barrel and no provision for a

Russian cavalry soldiers pose next to two small field guns in Manchuria, c.1904. They are armed with M1891 Dragoon rifles and three carry the M1881 Cossack *shaska*. They do not wear M1891 waist-belt pouches but carry their ammunition in a variety of chest bandoliers. (Photo by Harlingue/Roger Viollet/Getty Images)

bayonet – a reflection of the fact that, at the time, Russian military doctrine required the cavalry to conduct its hand-to-hand fighting with sabre or lance. Only in the United States were cavalry regarded as firearms-armed, mobile troops who could scout, screen and temporarily hold important objectives. In Europe, carbines were principally issued for guard duties or for guarding horses at grass. Their use as offensive weapons was purely incidental.

TOWARDS THE M1891/30

In the early 1920s, the new political regime in what was now the Soviet Union, having first established political stability and obedience to the centralized state, started to modernize its huge army. In 1922, the 11th Congress of the Communist Party of the Soviet Union considered that the Red Army should be halved to 800,000 men. By 1924, the Army's strength stood at 530,000 men. The M1891 rifle was subject to an upgrade in line with an international trend to produce a universal weapon for all troops. Germany's 7.92mm Mauser Kar 98k illustrates this trend well. All German soldiers who were armed with a rifle now had the Kar 98k, which prior to and during World War I would have been regarded as a carbine-length firearm for specialist troops.

In 1924, the Revolutionary Council of the Workers and Peasants' Red Army decided that the 33-year-old rifle should be modernized. The designers

Soviet Maxim M1910 machine-gun team in action. The loader carries his personal weapon – an M1891/30 rifle – slung across his back while serving the machine gun. The arrangement of the sling allows the rifle to rotate slightly during carriage, thus allowing the rifle to be carried flat side on to the body, leading to greater comfort. The crew wear *ushanka* hats and white snow-suits. The gun is on a typical Sokolov wheeled mount with shield, painted white for winter camouflage. (Courtesy of the Central Museum of the Armed Forces, Moscow via Stavka)

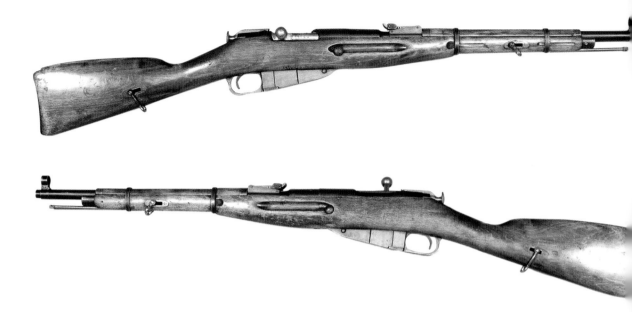

Two views of a Mosin-Nagant M1938 bolt-action carbine. This was an M1891/30 rifle with a much-shortened barrel and simplified rear sight. It would not accept a bayonet; a serious design flaw that was corrected with the folding spike-bayonet of the M1944. The short length of the M1938 carbine's barrel led to excessive recoil and muzzle blast when firing the powerful 7.62×54mmR cartridge. (Armémuseum/The Swedish Army Museum)

assigned to this task were E.K. Kabakov and I.A. Komaritskii. Troop trials commenced in 1927. The M1891 Dragoon was the basis for the new rifle and many were converted at this time. The barrel, shortened to 79cm, was protected by the traditional handguard and secured to the stock by two spring-retained rings, which made for easier maintenance in the field. The front sight was a simple piece of rod protected by a circular hood. It was dovetailed into the barrel and could be adjusted for windage. The rear sight was a modern tangent type, calibrated in metres rather than archaic and redundant *arshins*, while the rear sight aiming element was a simple notch. The charger was also simplified; and rather than the complicated spring steel 'fingers' that kept the cartridges in place, the ends of the sides of the charger were simply bent inwards to grip the cartridges. Other than that, the charger remained the same. The action and magazine remained unchanged. The buttplate was pressed steel and the webbing sling continued to be attached by small leather straps running through steel-lined slots.

In about 1928, the manufacturing process was simplified by making the receiver with a round breech rather than the original flat-sided 'hexagonal' one. The machining process also produced receivers with the left-hand-side wall of differing heights. Modern collectors term them 'high-wall' or 'low-wall' receivers (rather like the Winchester single-shot rifle of 1885, which had two distinctive designs). Standards of machining declined during the Great Patriotic War (1941–45), with the result that the cut on the wall was left higher to simplify production and enable rifles to be delivered more speedily to the front.

Design work was completed in the early months of 1930 and the new rifle was designated '7.62 Milimetrya Vintovka Obrasca 91/30 Goda' ('7.62 millimetre Rifle Model of the Year 1891/30'). It weighed 3.95kg and although at 123cm it was still long by modern European standards, it was much handier for the soldier than the M1891. Production commenced on 10 June 1930, and it is likely that use of the M1891/30 and the M1891 Dragoon rifles overlapped as old stocks of ammunition were used up.

Soviet infantry in a defensive position. The soldier in the immediate foreground is armed with an M1938 carbine. All of the soldiers wear the M1936 helmet with its distinctive crest. A variety of personal equipment is carried including gas-mask satchels and a *veshmeshok* rucksack. (From the fonds of the RGAKFD in Krasnogorsk via Stavka)

Later Mosin-Nagant variants

In 1938 a carbine was issued to Soviet troops, contrary to the general military doctrine of issuing a universal rifle that was suitable for all troops irrespective of role. The M1938 carbine replaced the M1907 version and featured a 51cm barrel and the M1891/30's hooded front sight and tangent rear sight. Somewhat bizarrely, it would not take the M1891/30 bayonet; but in 1944 this deficiency was rectified by fitting a folding spike-bayonet, which was locked in the 'fixed' position by means of a spring-loaded collar and folded back against the stock when not in use. It was a useful addition that gave specialist troops like mortar crews and artillerymen a hand-to-hand fighting capability if needed.

A Mosin-Nagant M1944 bolt-action carbine made at the Izhevsk Arsenal in 1944, with its bayonet in the stowed position. The addition of the folding spike-bayonet to what was simply an M1938 carbine gave its users a handy close-combat weapon that was readily deployed when needed. (NRA Museums, NRAMuseums.com)

Mosin-Nagant pouches and bandoliers

The advent of any new firearm with a different cartridge and loading system inevitably results in a new form of equipment to carry that ammunition. Because the Mosin-Nagant rifle represented the first time that the Russians had adopted a charger-loading small-bore rifle, existing pouches for the Berdan II single-shot rifle could not be used.

The existing ammunition pouch for the Berdan II held the single '4.2-line' cartridges in loops to present them to hand ready for loading. The pouch had a thin, rectangular top flap, hinged at the front, which opened away from the wearer's body and was secured in place by two straps running down its sides. Berdan II pouches are rarely encountered today, although specimens exist in museum collections and among some advanced collectors in Russia and Eastern Europe. Very good copies exist, made in the People's Republic of China, presumably for re-enactors.

Military Order No. 11 of 1881 required among other things that the Russian soldier be issued with a brown leather belt and two cartridge pouches. Contemporary pictures normally show the infantry wearing two pouches and the cavalry – which needed less ammunition – only one, on the right-hand side. Some infantrymen are shown with just one pouch, however, probably due to equipment shortages.

Any new pouch for the Mosin-Nagant rifle would have to accommodate cartridges held five at a time in steel chargers. A year after the introduction of the Mosin-Nagant, a new pattern of ammunition pouch was developed for it. The M1892 pouch was a smaller version of the Berdan II pouch with a small grasping tab sewn on the rear of the cover. It was made in chestnut-coloured brown leather and had two internal compartments separated by a divider. Its capacity was six five-round chargers. By wearing two pouches, the soldier now had ready use access to 60 cartridges; further ammunition was carried in the M1881 haversack to replenish that in the pouches as it was used. Armed Russian seamen and naval infantry had black leather pouches carried on the M1898 naval belt which appears to have been sometimes worn as a bandolier across the chest.

Military Order No. 51 of 1893 required the Russian soldier to carry additional ammunition in a canvas bandolier worn around the chest. Many nations adopted this practice, often storing chargers of cartridges in bandoliers in ammunition boxes so that they were immediately ready for use. Bandoliers for the Mosin-Nagant rifle tended to be produced locally from whatever colour canvas was to hand. White pouches from World War I and the Great Patriotic War (1941–45) are known, presumably to tone in with the white of snow suits.

The M1892 pouch was used throughout World War I and retained into the 1930s. This equipment put all of the load onto the soldier's hips, however, so the Soviets modified the pouch by the addition of a 'D' ring to allow shoulder-straps to be used. This was a better arrangement which transferred much of the load to the soldier's shoulders.

In 1937, the Soviet Union adopted a new style of twin-compartment pouch which carried 30 rounds. It was very similar to the German style of pouch, but it only had two rather than three compartments. The edges of the flaps were reinforced by rivets and the flaps themselves were secured by characteristic 'Y'-shaped closure straps.

Early in the Great Patriotic War, shortages of materials forced the Soviet authorities to issue pouches made from *kirsei* (rubberized canvas with a pebbled outer surface and black fabric inner). Brown leather was still used for the belt loops, securing straps and as bonding for the edges of the flaps. The securing straps were secured to the flaps by rivets, which simplified manufacture. Most of the Soviet pouches on the market today date from after 1945, but are essentially the same as those issued during the Great Patriotic War.

As the Great Patriotic War continued and raw materials became scarcer, pouches were made out of anything that came to hand – canvas, suede, leather-cloth, etc. Eventually, simple green canvas pouches (which looked like children's pencil cases) became the norm. Those with longer belt loops were used as magazine pouches and hung below the normal pouch to give a reserve ammunition supply. They normally held 20 cartridges in chargers of five. Pouches and bandoliers are also known to have been made out of captured German tent sections in splinter camouflage. Not surprisingly, a lack of standardization became the norm.

From 1939 onwards, the adoption of self-loading rifles such as the 7.62mm Tokarev SVT led to the production of pouches designed to carry spare magazines. One particularly ingenious pouch, first issued in 1942, could carry either two Tokarev self-loading rifle magazines, or four chargers of Mosin-Nagant cartridges, or a combination of the two. It did this by having folding internal dividers – transverse and lateral – that could be deployed according to the soldier's firearm.

After the Soviet victory in the Great Patriotic War, and with the recently established East Germany coming under strong Soviet influence, good-quality brown leather (sometimes pigskin) M1937 pouches were produced as war reparations in the early 1950s. These may be encountered with a smooth or pebbled finish and are internally marked with maker's name 'Lederwaren Zeitz VEB 1950', the Zeitz Leatherworks being a state-owned concern.

The People's Republic of China issued robust, if crudely made, green vinyl-covered canvas pouches for the 7.62mm Type 53 carbine. These held four chargers of cartridges, with no central divider. Other Warsaw Pact nations issued their own pouches, primarily made of brown leather.

Pouches for 7.62×54mmR Russian cartridges. Clockwise from top left: an M1891 pouch as used by the Imperial and early Soviet armies (this is a modern replica); a brown leather Soviet M1934 twin-compartment pouch (this example was made in East Germany in 1951 as war reparations); a People's Republic of China green leatherette pouch for the 7.62mm Type 53 carbine; a multi-purpose pouch to combine a combination of 7.62mm SVT-40 self-loading rifle magazines and chargers; a Soviet M1934 twin-compartment pouch made from *kirsei* (a leather substitute made from rubberized canvas); and a Soviet emergency pouch made from green canvas during the Great Patriotic War. (Author's Collection)

USE
The Mosin-Nagant enters service

INTO PRODUCTION

Unlike the French Lebel M1886 rifle, the issue of which was shrouded in secrecy by the ever-paranoid French military, the Russian Government did not appear to be concerned that the world knew that it had a adopted a modern rifle. In March 1896, British trade magazine *The Sporting Goods Review* carried a section entitled 'Notes on Military Arms' in which it reported 'Russia – The Mouzin or 3-Line rifle, M/91 with a caliber of 7.62 millimeters which is to supersede the single loading Berdan II. Rifle of 1871, caliber 10.66 millimeters (.42) is a magazine gun on the general lines of the Belgian Mauser.'

Russia sent a military mission to the French armaments factory at Châtellerault which had received a substantial production order to supplement a slow start to production at Russia's Tula, Izhevsk and Sestroryetsk arsenals. By 1902 some 3 million rifles had been made in Russia and the Russian Government considered that its rearmament programme was complete. Owing to the slow start to production in Russia, however, the M1891 was not fully issued to the majority of Russian troops until 1903 – by which time the Châtellerault factory had supplied 505,539 rifles – some 12 years after its adoption.

THE MOSIN-NAGANT IN THE RUSSO-JAPANESE WAR

The M1891 saw limited action during the Boxer Rebellion (1900) in the hands of armed seamen stationed at the Russian Legation in Peking. The new rifle's first widespread use was in the Russo-Japanese War (1904–05), although many Russian troops continued to be issued with the Berdan II rifle. This conflict was to see entrenchments and field fortifications assume

Siberian skirmishers of the Imperial Russian Army arrive in Liaoyang, site of the first major land battle of the Russo-Japanese War, 1904. These troops in full marching order carry M1891 rifles with fixed bayonets on their shoulders. They wear *shinel* greatcoats and sheepskin caps. Tent sections are worn *en banderole* across their chests; the ends are tucked into their characteristic copper pail-type mess-tins. (Photo by Culture Club/ Getty Images)

an even greater importance than they had during the Russo-Turkish War, as envisaged by I.S. Bloch, a Polish observer:

> Any advance in force, even in the loosest of formations, is absolutely out of the question on a front that is swept by the enemy's fire. Flank movements may be attempted, but the increased power that a magazine rifle gives to the defense will render it impossible for such movements to have the success that they formerly had. A small company can hold its own against a superior attacking force long enough to permit the bringing up of reinforcements. To attack any position successfully, it is estimated that the attacking force ought to outnumber the [defenders] by at least 8 to 1. It is calculated that 100 men in a trench would be able to put out of action 336 out of 400 soldiers who attacked them, while they were crossing a fire-zone only 300 yards wide. Certainly, everybody will be entrenched in the next war … The spade will be as indispensable to the soldier as his rifle. (Quoted in Wolff et al. 2007: 185)

Sure enough, the Russo-Japanese War on land witnessed the widespread use of field fortifications, as recounted by US Army officer John F. Morrison:

> Great reliance was placed on field intrenchments, and their use was very general. Once in the presence of an enemy the intrenching tool seemed next in importance to the rifle and ammunition. The rule on both sides seemed to be to always cover their positions with intrenchments as soon as taken up, even when held for only a short time. (Quoted in Wolff et al. 2007: 168fn)

Many of Russia's reservists had not encountered the Mosin-Nagant rifle before they were thrown into combat, as General Alexei Nikolayevich Kuropatkin – formerly Minister of War (1898–1904) under Tsar Nicholas II, and an ineffectual senior commander in the conflict – pointed out:

The result of the reinforcements being mobilized at different dates, contrary to my wishes, was that when the leading units reached the front, they has not settled down properly; the men did not know their officers, and *vice versâ*. Few corps had been able to do a musketry course, the 2nd Category reservists did not know the rifle, and hardly any had been tactically exercised, or if they had, it had been only for a few days. Divisions and corps had not been practised with the three arms [infantry, cavalry and artillery] ... The grounds for General [Minister of War Viktor Viktorovich] Sakharoff's opinion that newly raised reserve units only required two or three weeks to shake down instead of three and a half months are not obvious. Did he not know that the three-line rifle now in the possession of the army was quite new to the 2nd Category reservists? (Kuropatkin 1909: 273–77)

Later commentators have contrasted Russia's training regime unfavourably with that of their Japanese opponents:

The real Japanese strength lay in the infantry. With the invention earlier in the nineteenth century of breech-loading rifles using metallic cartridges, muskets and muzzle-loaders had been cast aside, but the Russians had not yet appreciated the true value of the new weapon. In training, they spent most of their ammunition rations on unobserved fire. The Japanese trained on the range. The Russians shot badly, the Japanese excellently. The Russians fired in volleys. The Japanese learned to aim and to shoot to kill. They were trained in close-quarters fighting, but they carried the bayonet in a scabbard and fixed it only to 'stack' rifles, or when about to go into hand-to-hand combat ... (Warner & Warner 2002: 167–68)

The shortage of ammunition also adversely affected training:

... the Russian marksmanship regulation allocated only twenty qualification rounds for mobilized troops. New recruits, in comparison, were allotted 125 rounds for annual range training. The pre-war Russian training manual also failed to address the improved range and accuracy of the new rifle, with half of the 125 rounds used for volley firing drills ...

In 1904, Russian infantry tactics still followed 19th Century lines, and had not progressed to match the capabilities of modern weapons ... When under fire, soldiers were to run while 'stooping', and use terrain for cover where possible. In the attack, Russian tactics called for the use of shock effect. Troops were to fire one rifle volley at the enemy followed by a bayonet charge. (Sisemore 2003: 71)

In action, the Russian infantry were often poorly handled. In appalling weather conditions, a Russian regiment was ordered to make a frontal attack with the bayonet: 'Of its twenty-three officers and 1,500 other ranks, one regiment lost twenty-one officers and 1,150 other ranks killed, wounded, or missing ... In this one action the First Siberian Rifle Corps lost a total of 6,000 men' (Warner & Warner 2002: 464). The Russian forces

Dug-in Russian troops armed with M1891 rifles with fixed bayonets await a Japanese attack during the Russo-Japanese War. The soldiers wear the lightweight summer uniform with peakless caps. NCOs kneel behind their men, ready to convey the orders of the standing officer with binoculars. During the Russo-Japanese War, Russia would lose large quantities of their new M1891 rifles to Japan. In Singapore, *The Straits Times* for 22 May 1906 detailed the Russian military stores captured by the Japanese, the contents of which included 110,548 rifles and 24,713,766 rounds of ammunition. No fewer than 70,000 captured rifles were exhibited outside the Imperial Palace in Tokyo during a military review, some of which would be issued for training purposes to universities and military academies during the 1920s and 1930s when there was a resurgence of militarism in Japan. In 1931, other captured rifles were issued to various Chinese warlords during the invasion of Manchuria. (Photo by Popperfoto/Getty Images)

won the battle, but the village they seized had no tactical value; and as machine guns began to arrive at the front, such assaults proved even more deadly to the attackers: 'One machinegun used by the Russians to defend Hei-kou-tai accounted for 180 men in a Japanese reserve company 220 men strong, while in the Russian attack on Pai-tai-tzu one Japanese gun was credited with causing a thousand casualties' (Warner & Warner 2002: 464).

In the event, the Russo-Japanese War was a humiliating defeat for Tsar Nicholas II's forces; while Russia's soldiers fought tenaciously, deep-seated logistical problems and command failures undermined their effectiveness on the battlefield. At the beginning of the conflict some 3.8 million M1891 rifles had been produced. As the war progressed, however, many of these rifles were either lost in action or captured. A combination of Russia's under-developed industrial base combined with the Byzantine bureaucracy of the Tsar's Ministry of War resulted in insufficient rifles being manufactured to replace those lost or damaged. There was always a desperate shortage of ammunition as well. As a consequence, the Imperial Russian General Staff set up a commission in 1910 to establish the causes of these shortfalls. The Polivanov Commission was commanded by General Aleksei Polivanov, who was also charged with establishing the size of Russia's supply and logistics framework that was needed to keep the Army properly supplied during wartime operations. The most important aspect of this was the size of the arms and munitions stockpile needed to support the Army in a European war. The Commission's report, delivered in late 1910, was based on three fundamental assumptions, all of which were based on the last war fought, rather than planning for the next war:

(1) Any future war would be short in duration, probably between two to six months but less than a year, even in the most extreme scenario.

(2) Logistic calculations were based on Russia's experience of the Russo-Japanese War and the location of potentially hostile nations.

(3) In the early phase of the war troops would be supplied from war-reserve stocks, giving factories an opportunity to increase production so that they could supply arms directly thereafter.

The result of the Polivanov Commission's report was that the Ministry of War allocated 3,924,323 M1891 rifles and 348,421 Berdan II rifles (4,272,744 in total) to war-reserve stocks. It is incredible to think that Russia still allocated significant numbers of long-obsolete, large-calibre, black-powder rifles to the reserve. They were probably intended for local militia or rear-area troops with limited territorial remits.

To keep costs down, production levels at the Imperial Russian arsenals were deliberately kept low. Initially, output was as little as 7 per cent of maximum theoretical capacity, although this rose to 12 per cent by 1913. Although it is easy with hindsight to see that output should have been raised in the years immediately preceding World War I, nobody seems to have understood the lessons of the Russo-Japanese War – a conflict in which previously unheard-of quantities of ammunition were expended.

THE MOSIN-NAGANT IN WORLD WAR I

Although the Russian Army duly learned some of the lessons of the Russo-Japanese War, there were important gaps in training, as one modern commentator has noted: 'The Russians were attempting to improve their infantry tactics along German principles, deploying strong skirmisher lines to conduct the fire-fight and bounding forward with squads and larger groups. Nevertheless, Russian marksmanship was bad; attacks were still too slow and generated too little firepower' (Zuber 2011: 98). The Germans themselves were disparaging about the marksmanship of the Russian infantrymen facing them in the early Eastern Front battles of World War I, as one divisional commander, Major-General Curt von Morgen, related:

> The Russian infantry has a great capability for marching ... the readiness of Russian infantry to establish field positions must be acknowledged. They are masters of the subject. The Russians are particularly skilled at defending woodland. Their marksmanship is generally bad. In one area however, the Russian infantry fails completely: in carrying out attacks. Clumsy by nature and poorly trained, the Russian is the opposite of a skilled rifleman. (Quoted in Buttar 2014: 410)

Fighting the production war

From the very first days of the M1891's adoption as Russia's new rifle, state arsenals struggled to keep up with demands to supply the rifle to the armed forces. In about 1910, Russia's peacetime Imperial Army establishment was just over 1,232,000 men. Initial mobilization added a further 2,533,000 to give a total of 3,765,000 men. This manpower total was within the war-reserve stocks of rifles total, but the difference was perilously small and did not really give sufficient leeway to replace those rifles lost in combat or training. More seriously, the figures did not allow for the maintenance of a sufficiently large reserve stockpile of rifles to deal with emergencies. As a consequence of this poor logistic planning, the Army was short of 870,000 rifles just two months after mobilization. Rifles were lost in the disastrous East Prussia campaign of August–September 1914 more quickly than they could be replaced. The catastrophic losses that occurred at the battles of Tannenberg and the Masurian Lakes simply aggravated what was an endemic problem. This deficiency characterized Russia's inefficient logistics throughout World War I.

The fully mobilized Army needed 5,500,000 rifles. A further 5,000,000 were needed to arm those conscripts called up during the war. Given that the Army lost some 200,000 rifles per month, combat losses over four years, calculated at 200,000 per month for 40 months of war, equated to 8,000,000 rifles, giving a total requirement during the war of 19,500,000 rifles. Russia procured a total of 11,392,000 rifles from all sources, which left a shortfall of no fewer than 8,108,000 rifles. Accordingly, Russia was forced to look overseas for the supply of rifles that, while not the M1891, would at least provide a battle-serviceable arm to supplement supplies. Among those considered to make up the shortfall was the Winchester Model 1895 lever-action rifle chambered for the 7.62×54mmR cartridge, used during the Brusilov Offensive of June–September 1916 when Austro-Hungarian forces counter-attacked Russian forces. Yet for all that the Winchester Model 1895 proved effective in defence, its mechanism was much more fragile and prone to jamming from ingress of dirt than the M1891's simple turn-bolt action.

Somewhat ironically, given the recent war between the two countries, Russia contracted with Japan to supply it with both the obsolescent Type 30 (1897) Arisaka rifle and the more up-to-date Type 38 (1905) Arisaka rifle and carbine. These weapons tended to end up in Russia's second-line forces, such as fortress troops or the Imperial Russian Navy; but the Arisaka was chambered for the 6.5×50mm cartridge, which further exacerbated supply problems. While exact totals are not known, it is estimated that Russia received some 600,000 Arisaka rifles and carbines. Russia also bought those 7mm Arisakas destined for Mexico which remained undelivered after the overthrow of President Victoriano Huerta's government in 1914.

The Remington Model 5 rolling-block rifle was simply the black-powder 11mm Model 1 brought into the 20th century by chambering it for a modern smokeless cartridge, normally 7×57mm, .303 or .30-40 Krag. The design adapted well to the

Two young Russian soldiers in field uniforms stand smartly to attention with their 6.5×50mm Arisaka Type 38 rifles and bayonets. The Japanese rifles' distinctive egg-shaped bolt knobs are finished bright and can be seen to the lower left. The soldiers each wear two M1891 ammunition pouches on waist belts with the Romanov eagle stamped on their buckles. Additional ammunition is carried in chest bandoliers. Some of the chargers have been inserted with the bullets uppermost, perhaps to show that these soldiers have plenty of ammunition and are ready to use it to defend their Tsar and Motherland. (Courtesy of the S.J. Perry Collection)

US contracts in World War I

The European Entente Powers soon realized that the scale of World War I would force them to look to the United States to supply them with arms as their domestic manufacturing capacities simply could not cope with demand. Accordingly, in 1915, the Russian Government contracted with the Remington Arms Company and the New England Westinghouse Company for 1,500,000 and 1,800,000 M1891 rifles and bayonets respectively at US$30 per unit. The Remington Union Metallic Cartridge Company was contracted to supply 1,000,000 cartridges.

Remington had a long history of arms manufacture; New England Westinghouse had no such track record, being accustomed to making heavy goods, but it transformed its production seamlessly to arms. Both factories invested heavily in new machinery. The rifles they produced were stocked in black American walnut, and tend to be of better quality than Russian-produced M1891s. American production can be distinguished by a small 'R' (Remington) and an 'H' with an arrow (New England Westinghouse) stamped on major components. Those M1891s made by Remington all bear the actual year of manufacture; those made by Westinghouse are all marked '1915' irrespective of when they were actually made.

The Russians insisted on sending inspectors to both factories to oversee build quality. In reality, they simply got in the way and dramatically reduced production:

> No sooner had the British contract (for Pattern 14 rifles) come under control than another of the allies came to Remington asking for arms to help fight the enemy, this time it was Russia, and the Czar's government also wanted a million rifles.

If the British contract had gone smoothly the Russian contract was the exact opposite. The official blueprints, master models and gauges all differed from another. Inspectors and fitters went mad trying to put parts together and test them. Every rifle had to be fitted by hand, with time-consuming filing and shaving. Instead of turning out 2,000 rifles a day, the Bridgeport plant was turning out 125. It was failing to meet its agreed deliveries and was losing a great deal of money in the process. It was an impossible situation. Remington engineers reworked the official Russian standards and finally obtained official approval from the Czar's representatives. (Canfield 2010: 297)

One such Russian inspector was a huge Cossack captain who wore full costume and was nicknamed by the workforce, 'Alexander the Great'. Alexander used to test the sears of loaded rifles by banging them on hard concrete. He apparently wrote off upwards of a dozen rifles a day. Seeking revenge for this wanton vandalism, the workforce gave Alexander a finely filed rifle with a sear that just held the striker when cocked. He duly banged the rifle butt on the ground and it went off, the bullet perforating a water main in the ceiling. Alexander was nearly drowned and had to be rescued from the torrent of icy water, but the incident soon put a stop to his escapades. Whether this story is true or apocryphal, it serves to illustrate the atmosphere of mistrust and interference created by the Russian inspectors. The overcoming of this by Remington employees was a major achievement in itself.

The Central Powers were keen to see the Remington and New England Westinghouse production halted and the supply of rifles to the Allies stemmed. The Ambassador of the Imperial German

Government to the United States, Count Johann Heinrich von Bernstorff, protested that America was behaving in an 'unneutral' manner by supplying rifles. Given the strength of anti-German feeling since the U-boat sinking of the British ocean liner RMS *Lusitania* on 7 May 1915, in which 128 of 139 US passengers died and which precipitated the United States' entry into World War I, his protests fell upon deaf ears. The Count also accused the US of supplying 'dum-dum' ammunition – a claim that was quite unfounded. Attempts to foment strikes at the factory in Bridgeport, Connecticut failed, mainly because the workforce was well paid and had access to cheap housing.

The future of the Remington and New England Westinghouse workforces came under serious threat as a result of the October Revolution of 1917 and the fall of Tsar Nicholas II. The new and democratically elected Russian Provisional Government of Alexander Fyodorovich Kerensky defaulted on payments for foreign arms, and the ensuing Soviet regime followed suit – unsurprising given that it was bankrupt and wanted to opt out of the war. Both Remington and New England Westinghouse were now in severe financial trouble. Marcellus Dodge (1881–1963), the chairman of Remington's board of directors, who had even used his own money to back the company, said: 'Every night when I tried to go to sleep, I lay there thinking that I had nothing left of all I owned, and that I had no further employment for the thousands of men who had worked hard and loyally during the days of stress' (quoted in Hatch 1972: 223).

In order to try to save the factories, some quick political footwork in a Congressional Committee by the Chief of Ordnance, Brigadier General Charles B. Wheeler, ensured that the US Government bought much of the remaining inventory at an average price of US$21.50 for each rifle – about two-thirds of the original contract price. The deal led in turn to 1918's Urgent Deficiency Appropriation Bill. The cash bail-out – even though much reduced – kept both companies afloat and saved jobs.

The M1891 rifle in US Government service was designated 'US Magazine Rifle Caliber 7.62mm, Model of 1916'. US-procured M1891s are among the rarest of US martial arms. They are recognizable by their good condition, plus the 'eagle head', 'flaming bomb' and US Ordnance stamps in the stock, immediately in front of the magazine floor-plates.

Statistics for the delivery of M1891 rifles by the United States are unreliable. The US firearms authority Bruce Canfield estimates that Remington supplied about 750,000 to 840,000 units, with production peaking at 4,000 rifles a day. Similarly, he ascribes a figure of about 770,000 to New England Westinghouse. Using Canfield's figures, the total would be in the region of 1,520,000 to 1,160,000. Another US authority puts the total as high as 2 million (Mercaldo et al. 2011: 53).

7.62×54mmR cartridge, as it did to the 8mm Lebel M1886 cartridge. France, also short of rifles, bought some 50,000 Model 5s as a stopgap; the Russian total is not known but is likely to have been of a similar number to that of the French.

Some idea of the scale of Russia's shortage of riles can be gathered from the testimony of General Vladimir Alecksay Sukhomlinov (1848–1926) during his trial for treason in 1916. Sukhomlinov was Minister of War in 1909–15 and repeatedly assured the *Duma* (Russian Parliament) that there was an adequate supply of *matériel* to the troops, in the face of strong evidence to the contrary. Bowing to public pressure, Tsar Nicholas II impeached and tried him for treason. During his trial, Sukhomlinov admitted that there were only sufficient rifles to arm one in ten soldiers. Unarmed men would have to take the rifles of casualties. Sukhomlinov was convicted and sentenced to penal service. He was released to Finland by Soviet amnesty in 1921, and died there in 1926.

The Mosin-Nagant in Central Powers service

The use of captured enemy war *matériel* has been a well-established practice since the earliest days of organized warfare. After the East Prussian campaign, Germany found itself with thousands of captured and perfectly serviceable enemy Mosin-Nagant rifles and ammunition. The battle of Tannenberg in August 1914 left 78,000 Russian soldiers dead and a further 92,000 prisoners of war. A month later, the first battle of the Masurian Lakes saw 125,000 Russians killed, wounded or missing and 45,000 taken into captivity. It is easy to envisage the large numbers of captured Russian rifles resulting from these levels of casualties.

The Germans made enthusiastic use of captured enemy rifles (*Beutegewehren*) – the Army's 50th, 52nd, 54th and 56th divisions were all armed with captured Mosin-Nagants – because this freed up arsenals to produce Mauser rifles and carbines for use at the front. Troops behind the front line who still needed to be armed, found themselves increasingly equipped with *Beutegewehren*. M1891s especially were used to arm whole Landsturm (Home Guard) battalions and naval infantry divisions; ambulance-drivers, military railway troops, coastal gunners, airship troops and recruits in training establishments were also recipients of captured Mosin-Nagants.

The distribution of captured rifles among Germany's naval forces started within the first months of the war. On 6 November 1914, the Secretariat for the Imperial Navy wrote to every naval command to say that as the demand for Gewehr 98s by the Army had been so extraordinary, it was no longer possible to deliver these rifles to the Navy. Instead, arrangements had been made for 10,000 captured French rifles (probably Gras M1874 and Lebel M1866/93) and 7,000 captured Russian rifles to be provided to naval personnel. Mauser Gewehr 98 rifles already in German Navy service were ordered to be withdrawn – in truth, their issue for shipboard use was not an efficient use of resources because rifles were only used occasionally – and replaced by *Beutegewehren* that proved just as effective and released many Gewehr 98s for infantry service on the Western Front.

On 1 October 1915, stocks of captured Russian rifles held by the Kiel dockyard alone stood at 9,705. Machine guns which had been issued to U-boats for mine detonation were withdrawn and each was replaced with two captured Russian rifles. The latter in fact proved more suitable for the task and used less ammunition. Every ship in the Baltic Fleet was issued with three captured rifles for detonating mines. By February 1918, the Kiel dockyard stock of captured Russian rifles had been reduced to 4,405.

The extent of German use of captured Mosin-Nagants is apparent by their appearance in significant numbers of contemporary photographs of German military personnel. Some M1891s were rechambered for the 7.92×57mm Mauser cartridge, but most were simply issued with captured 7.62×54mmR cartridges because of the huge quantities that were readily available. M1891s issued to the German Navy are generally marked on their buttplates, the basic marking being the square Imperial crown over a large 'M' (Marine). This is in addition to more specialized unit markings, of which the following have been observed:

MD (Matrosen-Division – Naval Division)
SB (See-Bataillon – Marines)
TD (Torpedo-Division – technical personnel for torpedo boats)
WK (Werft-Kiel – Kiel dockyard)
WW (Werft-Wilhelmshaven – Wilhelmshaven dockyard)

As Germany's ally, Austria-Hungary's forces also received large numbers of captured Russian rifles, as did Turkish forces. Surviving examples are rare, probably because so many German small arms were destroyed in accordance with the terms of the Treaty of Versailles (1919). Italy received many M1891s from Austria-Hungary as war reparations in the 1920s and sold them on to Finland. Known examples have regimental stamps on their buttplates and the words 'Deutsches Reich' surrounding a German eagle stamped over the original Romanov eagle on their butts. Those that were refurbished at government arsenals prior to reissue are marked 'AZR' if German and 'AH' if Austro-Hungarian.

Beutegewehren tended to be used with their captured socket-bayonets, although some conversions to Mauser-style knife-bayonets were undertaken. Most of the *Beutegewehren* that were converted received a tubular adapter which was screwed to the muzzle so that an *ersatz* (substitute) steel-hilted bayonet could be fixed. If the adapter was not used, the stock was modified with a Mauser bayonet bar secured by a conventional Gewehr 98 nose cap. The Germans soon recognized the impracticality of keeping the bayonet on the rifle and issued tubular steel scabbards. The Austrians issued either a leather scabbard or one which seems to have been adapted from a converted French Lebel bayonet scabbard.

Studio portrait of a Russian cavalry soldier armed with a 7.62mm Winchester Model 1895 rifle and an M1881 *shaska*. Winchester was able to tool up for speedy delivery of the Russian contract because it already produced its NRA Musket model in .30-06, which had the same bore diameter as 7.62mm. All that was necessary for the Russian contract was to use a 7.62×56mmR chamber reamer and install the specially designed charger-loading guides. Note how the soldier wears his sword in the Oriental manner, with the cutting edge towards the rear. (From the fonds of the RGAKFD in Krasnogorsk via Stavka)

The Mosin-Nagant in the 'Polar Bear Expedition'

The United States issued many of its Remington and New England Westinghouse M1891s for training, to the Colorado and Alaskan National Guards, a militia unit named the 'US Guards' and to the Student Army

Training Corps. A substantial number were issued to US forces serving in North Russia as part of the American North Russian Expeditionary Force (popularly known as the Polar Bear Expedition). US forces had been deployed to Archangel, Murmansk and Vladivostok to protect US property and interests from the 'Reds' (Bolshevik Communists) during the Russian Civil War (1917–22). The US sided with the 'Whites' (Imperialist forces). It was believed that issuing US-made Russian rifles to US forces in Russia would facilitate ammunition supply as 7.62mm cartridges were available locally.

Mention is made of these rifles by Lieutenant John Cudahy of Company B, 339th Infantry Regiment, serving with the Polar Bear Expedition, who led a successful attack on Communist forces at Tulgas, near Archangel. In his 1924 book *Archangel: the American war with Russia, by a chronicler*, Cudahy recalls that:

The main body of the enemy had carried with them far up the river to Kotlas and down the railway to Vologda, rations, rifles, guns and ammunitions, American manufactured ... But most disheartening of all were the Russian rifles issued to the infantry. They were manufactured in our country by the million for use of the Imperial Army; long, awkward pieces, with flimsy bolt mechanisms, that frequently jammed. These weapons had never been targeted by the Americans, and their sighting systems were calculated in Russian paces instead of yards. They had a low velocity and were thoroughly unsatisfactory. The unreliability of the rifle, prime arm of the infantry, was an important factor in the lowering of Allied morale ... (Cudahy 1924: 63)

This US 'Doughboy' in shirtsleeves has a US-made M1891 rifle. He is pictured during basic training in 1918 after the US Ordnance had bought numerous M1891 rifles from Remington and New England Westinghouse to safeguard the companies and their workforces after the Russians defaulted on contracts following the October Revolution of 1917. He wears the 'Montana' campaign hat, semi-breeches and canvas gaiters above ankle boots. (Tom Laemlein / Armor Plate Press)

Archangel, April 1919 (opposite)

This plate depicts some of the desperate fighting between US forces and Bolsheviks ('Reds') near the village of Bolshie Ozerki. The US soldier carries an M1891 rifle with fixed bayonet. He wears a fur cap, greatcoat, padded overboots and the M1910 rifleman's belt with suspenders.

The wounded Bolshevik lying at the American's feet carries the Dragoon version of the M1891 rifle. This had a slightly shorter barrel and a simpler rear sight than the infantry rifle. He carries his ammunition in a single M1891 pouch and is clad in the distinctive uniform adopted by the fledgling Red Army. This includes the *budenovka* broadcloth helmet and greatcoat with red spearpoint-shaped, appliqué cloth patches to the front, ostensibly inspired by the 17th-century *Strelsky* uniform.

The dismounted, charging cavalryman about to attack the American also carries an M1891 rifle with fixed bayonet. He retains the old Tsarist uniform with a peaked cap and carries his ammunition in a cloth bandolier about his chest. He is also armed with an M1881 Dragoon *shaska* single-edged sword worn in the Oriental manner with the cutting edge to the rear. Its scabbard has mounts to carry his bayonet when the latter is not in use.

Soldiers of the American North Russian Expeditionary Force – the so-called Polar Bear Expedition – pose for a photograph to celebrate the end of the war with Russia in 1920. US-made M1891s, three of which are piled in front of the American flag, were issued in order to facilitate ammunition supply, but the American troops were not well-disposed to the Russian rifles and lamented the loss of their M1903 Springfields and Pattern M1917s. (Tom Laemlein / Armor Plate Press)

Cudahy continues: 'In the snow, rifles became clogged in the breeches, so that the bolts would not drive home, and men had to dig them clean with fingers stiffening from cold, but still, a little at a time, the attack wormed on and on ... At the end of three hours snow clogging in rifle breeches has frozen solid and they can shoot no more ...' (Cudahy 1924: 114). His assessment of the M1891 appears to be larded with prejudice. Put bluntly, he (and many other US troops) did not like them simply because they were not M1903 Springfields or Pattern 1917 rifles. The assertion that the M1891 was 'flimsy' is wholly unfounded; quite the opposite was the case: the M1891 was nothing if not robust and 'soldier proof'. Any rifle is likely to jam in sub-zero conditions, as frozen fingers on the part of the shooter do not make any positive contribution to good weapon handling. Freezing snow clogging the breech could happen to any bolt-action rifle. As for the allegation of low velocity, the 7.62×54mmR cartridge is ballistically similar to the .30-06 cartridge. Perhaps local ammunition supplies were unreliable and led to Cudahy's claim.

A British Army officer, Lieutenant-Colonel John Ward of 26th (Service) Battalion (3rd Public Works Pioneers), The Duke of Cambridge's Own (Middlesex Regiment), makes an interesting observation: 'A Magyar soldier seeing Kalmakoff with his Ataman banner borne by his side, took a point-blank shot at his head, but he forgot the high trajectory of the old Russian rifle, and the bullet merely grazed the top of the Cossack leader's head and sent his papaha [fur hat] into the mud' (Ward 1920). Ward's 1920 book, *With the Die-Hards in Siberia*, is one of only a few contemporary accounts of the British presence in North Russia. Ward (who was made a Companion of the Bath by the British Crown and an ataman by his Cossack allies) was an experienced soldier, so his comment about the M1891's 'high trajectory' is bizarre: most military rifles shoot high with battle sights at short ranges. The reason for the miss does not appear to have had anything to do with the M1891's sights. Perhaps the Magyar was simply a bad shot.

BETWEEN THE WORLD WARS

The Mosin-Nagant in the USA after World War I

At the end of World War I, the victorious powers were awash with surplus military arms. The United States had bailed out the Remington and New England Westinghouse companies by purchasing defaulted Russian contracts to keep those companies financially solvent; but the M1891 rifle had never been popular in the United States, largely due to nationalistic prejudices which favoured US-designed service rifles. In terms of finish and engineering it was inferior to the much-loved M1903 Springfield and Pattern 1917 rifles. What, then, to do with the thousands of US-made M1891 rifles in the US Government inventory?

The US Government, through the auspices of the Office of the Director of Civilian Marksmanship, sold M1891s to civilians for the attractive price of US$3 each; but even at such a bargain-basement price, civilian target shooters shied away from the rifle. To their eyes the M1891 was antiquated to look at, had sights calibrated in unfamiliar foreign units and used a 'foreign' cartridge that was not the tried and trusted .30-06.

The New York arms dealer Francis Bannerman Sons purchased many thousands of the M1891s, probably at less than the US$3 asking price. Bannerman's was an enigma which catered for genuine Army-surplus markets and which also encouraged the collector and amateur military historian. The founder, Francis Bannerman VI (1851–1918), was long dead when his sons Frank and David offered Mosin-Nagants and ammunition in their 1927 sales catalogue.

A sporterized version with a new .30-06 barrel was US$10.45, which was very cheap for a serviceable hunting rifle. The full military version, advertised as suitable for 'American Legion' and other firing squads, cost US$14.00 each. They, too, had been altered to .30-06. Received wisdom has it that these conversions are inherently dangerous to use (anyone intending to use any former military rifle should have it checked by a competent gunsmith); but having examined one, the author could not find any feature that was unsound. Original 7.62mm ammunition was US$2.50 per 100, US$1 cheaper than the equivalent number of .30-06 cartridges.

In 1926, the ammunition maker Remington Union Metallic Cartridge Company sought to capitalize on the large numbers of M1891 rifles in the United States by providing a cartridge suitable for hunting. *The American Rifleman* carried the following advert in its issue of 15 June 1926: 'There are thousands of 7.62 m-m Russian military rifles in the hands of American sportsmen, but until recently there has been no ammunition suitable for game shooting for those riflemen.' Remington offered the 7.62×54mmR cartridge with a 150-grain (9.72g) bronze-point expanding bullet. Its ballistics were given as 2,800ft/sec (855m/sec) generating 2,620ft-lb (3,552 joules) of kinetic energy.

Paradoxically, despite the large numbers of M1891 rifles released onto the market in the United States during the 1920s and 1930s, an original US Ordnance-marked M1891 rifle is a scarce collector's item today.

The Mosin-Nagant in Spain 1936–39

The Spanish Civil War (1936–39) saw the use of a great number of imported firearms of all types, and both the Nationalist and Republican forces were particularly desperate for relatively modern rifles. The list of the different makes and models of rifles is staggering and reads like an arms dealer's sales catalogue. Europe unloaded all of its obsolete and often worn-out rifles on Spain, usually in exchange for hard currency. Unsurprisingly, the M1891 was found in Spain in significant numbers and was the most numerous foreign rifle supplied to the Republicans. George Orwell (1903–50) recalls Mosin-Nagant rifles in his book *Homage to Catalonia*:

> It was not only that they were picked men physically, it was their weapons that most astonished me. All of them were armed with brand-new rifles of the type known as 'the Russian rifle' (these rifles were sent to Spain by the U.S.S.R., but were, I believe, manufactured in America). I examined one of them. It was a far from perfect rifle, but vastly better than the dreadful old blunderbusses we had at the front. (Orwell 1938)

Orwell was partially right, in that the M1891 rifles were from the surplus stock built by Remington and New England Westinghouse for the Tsarist Government during World War I. After World War I, some 5,000 of these rifles were sold to Mexico; and because the Mexican Government sympathized with the Republican side in the Spanish Civil War, it sent its rifles and cartridges to Spain. Examples of these US-made Mosin-Nagants were undoubtedly what were seen by Orwell in Barcelona during the Telephone Exchange siege of May 1937, but he confuses them with brand-new M1891/30 rifles bought from the Soviet Union. (Despite having signed the Non-Intervention Agreement in August 1936, the Soviet Union continued to sell large quantities of military equipment to the Republicans.) Contrary to popular belief, these rifles were not supplied *gratis* to aid a fellow left-wing government in the struggle against international fascism; they were paid for with gold bullion from the Bank of Spain's reserves.

An unnamed soldier of the XV International Brigade (in all probability an American in the Abraham Lincoln Battalion) also recalls seeing Mosin-Nagants. In February 1937 he was in the Republican city of Albacete in Castilla-La Mancha, headquarters of the International Brigades:

> In the chill February evening they lined up behind a supply truck and unloaded heavy boxes about the size of coffins. Breaking them open, they found new bolt action rifles, each wrapped in Mexico City newspapers and oozing Cosmoline. With each came a small cloth bag stuffed with cleaning brushes and small tools but no rags. 'Clean them,' came the order. 'With what?' came a plaintive voice. 'Use your shirt-tails,' barked Seacord. The rifles were Remingtons, some barrels stamped with the Czarist double-eagle, others with the Soviet hammer and sickle. The latter were seven centimetres shorter and a few ounces lighter, but their bolts were prone to jam when overheated. (Some rifles were stamped 'Made in Connecticut.') The men nicknamed their rifles 'Mexicanskis' and the story passed into local folklore that they had

A Spanish Republican soldier – probably serving in the International Brigades – carries his M1891/30 rifle over his shoulder. As proper slings were often not available, soldiers improvised from available cloth and the sling strap slots were often fitted with crude, heavy wire loops as in this case. Contrary to popular belief, these rifles were not a gift from the Soviet Union to aid the Republican struggle; they were paid for with gold bullion from the Bank of Spain's reserves. (Tom Laemlein / Armor Plate Press)

been manufactured in the United States, sent to the Czar in 1914, copied by Bolshevik artisans, sold to Mexico for revolutionary work and then donated to the Spanish Republic. Some had leather slings, the rest only flimsy linen ones. (Eby 2007)

The Seacord referred to here was Lieutenant Doug Seacord, commander of the Abraham Lincoln Battalion's machine-gun company. He was killed in February 1938. William Herrick, also of the Abraham Lincoln Battalion's machine-gun company, has a similar recollection:

As he spoke we could see large wooden crates stacked beside him. He ordered them opened. Brand new rifles, still covered with cosmoline. Russian carbines. (Some later said they were Mexican; I don't know.) We yipped in glee. We cheered. We laughed. We waved our hands against the sky. Long live the Soviet Union. Long live Comrade Stalin. Long live the Frente Popular. Long live Comrade Marty. Thank God, we're gonna have guns. Each had a long, slender tri-bladed bayonet. They were frightening – the thought of one entering your body, the thought of slamming one into the body of an enemy. We were given helmets, gas masks, cartridge belts with bullets. Now we were real soldiers. We cheered again. (Herrick; no date)

Another International Brigader, the Irish political activist Michael O'Riordan, recalled:

And there we got our first rifles. Russian rifles and we were told not to say a word about the Russian rifles, so we fell in with that, we called them Mexicanski rifles and even today you can hear an International

Brigader refer to the Mexicanski rifles, it's the Russian rifles he's talking about because we were very good in that sense of keeping military secrets. (O'Riordan 2009)

As a result, any Mosin-Nagant rifle with Spanish provenance is called a 'Mexicanski'. Their issue was confined to the International Brigades, probably for logistical reasons due to the lack of interchangeability of the 7.62mm cartridge with the 7×57mm Mauser cartridge of the Ejército Popular de la República (People's Republican Army). There are numerous contemporary photographs of International Brigaders armed with 'Mexicanskis', the rifles being readily identifiable by their length and permanently fixed spike-bayonets. The Abraham Lincoln Battalion of the XV International Brigade carried them at the battle of Jarama in February 1937, as did the British Battalion's Major Attlee Company (named after British Labour Party leader Clement Attlee) at the battle of the Ebro in July 1938.

Figures for the number of Mosin-Nagants sent to Spain by the Soviet Union vary. The Russian scholar Iurii E. Ribalkin puts the number at 497,813 with 862 million rounds of ammunition; the historian Gerald Howson's estimate is 292,645 to 379,645; and a Soviet estimate issued in 1974 specifies 337,793. Irrespective of the true total, it is fair to say that hundreds of thousands of Mosin-Nagants were sold to the Republicans by the Soviet Union.

The unnamed soldier's comment about the bolts of the M1891/30 rifles jamming when hot is not repeated in any other source of which the author is aware. Indeed, modern firing trials failed to replicate this phenomenon. A consideration of the simple physics suggests that the jams were caused by other factors than heat – probably poor maintenance by inexperienced personnel. As the barrel and receiver heat up during sustained firing they expand, making the locking lugs on the bolt fractionally looser. To cause a jam, the bolt head would have to expand while the receiver remained dimensionally the same, causing the lugs to bind. That is not possible. Heat transfer is uniform, with both the bolt head and receiver expanding at the same rate as the temperature rises.

William Rust, a British member of the XV International Brigade, recalls the inspecting divisional general upbraiding the men for dirty rifles and warning them that such weapons were more dangerous to the firer than the enemy. Poor maintenance and erratic cleaning appear to have been recurring problems during the Spanish Civil War, owing to a constant lack of materials; some of it was probably due to the lackadaisical attitude of the men, however. As they were mainly untrained idealists and not professional soldiers, the instinct to keep their rifles in good order to help ensure their survival was not strong.

A small number of authentic 'Mexicanskis' are known to collectors. They tend to be in well-worn condition and their stocks sometimes bear a small flaming grenade ordnance mark impressed by the Spanish after the war. The sling slots are often filled with improvised wire swivels to allow conventional European-type slings to be used, rather than the Soviet ones secured by small leather straps.

Finnish Mosin-Nagant rifles

The Mosin-Nagant rifles developed and issued by Finland are the most distinctive and have the greatest variation, as the Finns adapted the basic Russian design to meet their own requirements during the 1920s and 1930s. It is important to remember that the development of the Finnish Mosin-Nagant rifle tended to be based on the wishes and requirements of at least three distinctive bodies – the Finnish Army (Suomen Armeija), the Civil Guard (Suojeluskunta) and – up until its dissolution in 1934 – the White Guard.

Finland had been an autonomous Grand Duchy of the Russian Empire since 1809. After the October Revolution in 1917, there was great political uncertainty as to who formed the governing executive of the country, which declared its independence from Russia on 1 December 1917. The resultant Civil War, fought from 27 January to 15 May 1918, resulted in 39,000 deaths, with atrocities and acts of terror committed by both the Red and the White factions. After gaining its independence from the Soviet Union, Finland continued to develop and issue many types of Mosin-Nagant rifle, from standard Russian examples to others that had been completely reworked into distinctive Finnish types.

The Soviet invasion of Finland on 30 November 1939 and the ensuing Winter War (ending on 13 March 1940) saw further supplies of Mosin-Nagant rifles being made available to the Finns as a result of the heavy losses of men and *matériel* suffered by the Red Army. Peace lasted for just over a year before the Finns were again at war with the Soviet Union in the Continuation War, which raged from 25 June 1941 to 19 September 1944. The terms of the armistice imposed by the Soviets were harsh. As well as paying massive monetary reparations, the Finns ceded territory to the Soviets, but retained their independence.

The M/24, dubbed *Lottakivääri* ('Lotta's Rifle') in acknowledgement of the work carried out by the *Lotta Svärd* women's auxiliary of the Finnish Civil Guard to purchase and repair some 10,000 rifles as part of the war effort, was the result of an extensive and ambitious Finnish upgrading of

A 7.62mm M/27 bolt-action rifle. The M/27 was a Finnish conversion of the long and unwieldy Mosin-Nagant M1891 rifle. The barrel was shortened to 68.5cm and a pair of protective 'ears' was added to the front sight. (The original rear sight was retained but re-graduated.) A new forend cap for a knife-bayonet was fitted, reinforced by two 'lolly-stick' plates. A side sling loop was fitted and the stock was pierced with a Mauser Gewehr 98-style slot. The bolt was fitted with a turned-down handle and the stock was given a corresponding scoop under it. The sling slot in the butt was filled in and a brass marker disc added. (NRA Museums, NRAMuseums.com)

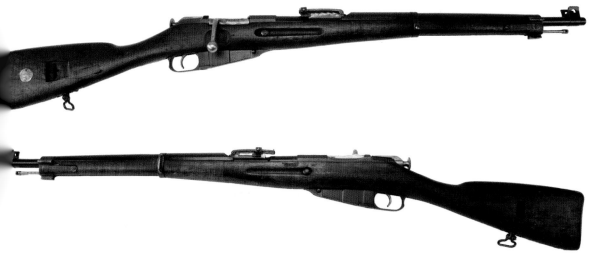

A youthful Finnish Civil Guard soldier with a captured M1891 rifle. He wears a World War I-era German M1916 steel helmet with its distinctive lugs for the reinforcing brow plate. The M1916 was one of the most common types of helmet used by the Finn in the Winter War. He wears the Civil Guard badge of an 'S' (Suojeluskunta) surmounted by fir twigs against a bi-coloured background, incorporating the colours of his district. (Photo by Keystone-France/Gamma-Keystone via Getty Images)

the Mosin-Nagant M1891 rifle. International involvement in the project included the manufacture of new barrels in Germany (13,000) and Switzerland (8,000). Barring the first 3,000 barrels manufactured by SIG in Switzerland, all were heavier and stepped at the muzzle end, this latter feature enabling the fitting of the M1891 bayonet. Other modifications included the improvement of the trigger pull by virtue of a coil spring wrapped around the trigger pin. The Civil Guard mark of three fir-tree springs over the letter 'S' was applied to all M/24s.

In 1927, the Ordnance Department of the Finnish Ministry of Defence proposed a considerable reworking of the Mosin-Nagant M1891 rifle. The most notable change was the fitting of a new and heavier 68.5cm barrel to replace the M1891's 80cm barrel. Other changes included the addition of two 'ears' to protect the front sight; the addition of 'wings' to the bolt-connecting bars; and changes to the stock and the barrel channels to take the new barrel. The existing socket bayonet was replaced by a knife-bayonet.

With some 50,000 M/27s having been produced against a projected total of 120,000 units, problems with the new barrel bands and shortened stock led to steps being taken to strengthen the M/27, and these changes were duly incorporated in new-production rifles and retrofitted to existing units. Production ran from mid-1927 to 1940, and the M/27 saw considerable and effective use during the Winter War. A small number of cavalry carbines (about 2,000) were made, but very few survive.

The M/28 was designed by and for the White Guard paramilitary militia, and can be distinguished from the M/27 by virtue of a modified trigger and a hinged barrel.

In the early 1930s, successful development of a new rear sight to replace that of the M/28 led in turn to initial production in 1932–33 of what was designated the M/28-30. Other than replacement of the M/28's 'Konovalov' rear sight, small changes were made to the hand guard and the magazine. Further modifications were incorporated in M/28-30s produced between 1934 and 1941, including changes to the front sight, the use of Finnish steel for the barrel, and the fitting of an aluminium sleeve to counter excess heat.

The M/28-30 was the rifle used by legendary sniper Simo Häyhä (1905–2002) on the Kollaa front during the Winter War. Known by the Soviets as 'White Death', during a 100-day period he was credited with an astonishing 505 kills. Häyhä preferred to conduct his sniping duties from the seated position for better stability; and he favoured open (as opposed to telescopic) sights because they allowed him to adopt a lower profile in the snow. His rifle, No. 60974, is now displayed with Häyhä's uniform in the Heritage Museum of the North Karelian Infantry Brigade in Joensuu, Finland.

The M/30 rifle, produced by Tikkakoski in 1943 and 1944, was an improved Mosin-Nagant M1890/30 that made use of parts stripped from some of the nearly 125,000 M1891/30s captured from the Red Army during the Winter War and the Continuation War. This considerable spares source was augmented by the purchase of a further 57,000 examples, this time from Germany's stocks of captured rifles. M/30s in Finnish service featured solid and two-piece stocks; and Finnish blade and Soviet hooded-post front sights are known.

The M/39 – nicknamed *Ukko-Pekka* ('Old Man Pete') after former President of Finland, Pehr Evind Svinhufvud (1861–1944) – shared many features with the M28/30, betraying the fact that the M/39 was the result of a compromise between the Finnish Army and the White Guard as they strove for a design that could form the basis of standardized production. Features included new (cut-down M91) barrels, improved barrel bands, a double swing swivel and (in early-production rifles) a 'straight' stock. Production was undertaken by SAKO and VKT and ran to 102,000 units, the last of which came off the line during the 1960s.

Even though Finland adopted the Valmet assault rifle in 1962, the Mosin-Nagant design survived as a specialist rifle in Finnish military service well into the 1980s. One such weapon was the M/28-76 target rifle, based on modified M/28-30 and M/39 rifles and produced in two versions by the Finnish Army. Another specialist weapon was the Tarkkuuskivääri (Tkiv) 85 sniping rifle, designed around original Mosin-

A Finnish soldier shows his rifle to English press photographer Eric Calcraft (at left). The Finn wears a white balaclava helmet and field cap with a sheepskin coat. His rifle appears to have been sporterized and he may have been a hunter. Many Finns enjoyed hunting and the outdoor life which gave them a head start in fieldcraft and camouflage over the invading Soviets, who were at a disadvantage in the snowy Finnish forests. (Photo by Carl Mydans/The LIFE Picture Collection/Getty Images)

Winter War, 1939–40 (overleaf)

Finnish troops engage a column of Soviet infantry. Unusually, both Finns have opted to fix bayonets, indicating that they are expecting close-quarter combat. They are well equipped for winter warfare with snowsuits and Lappland (ski) boots. The emphasis is on practicality and comfort. By contrast, the Soviets are equipped to fight in more temperate climates and make easy targets as they flounder in the deep snow.

The kneeling Finnish rifleman fires at the Soviets with his Mosin-Nagant M/27 rifle. This was a Finnish rework of the original Russian rifle with replacement barrel, altered sights and a native Arctic birch stock. It carries a knife-bayonet rather than the original socket type. He wears a German steel helmet and German-inspired three-section ammunition pouches. He carries a *puukko* personal hunting knife of traditional design. His comrade carries a restocked and rebuilt Russian M1891 rifle with its original socket-bayonet. Unlike the Soviets he has a scabbard for it, preferring to carry it at his waist when not in use, rather than permanently fixed on the rifle.

The claws of the lion: a 7.62mm M/39 rifle. This was perhaps the most advanced of all the Mosin-Nagant rifle versions and featured a newly designed stock, sights and sling points. The stock is made from three separate pieces of Arctic birch, which did not warp in low temperatures. The lower portion of the butt is spliced together (reminiscent of the Japanese Arisaka rifle) and the forend is spliced to the rear portion in front of the rear-sight bed. (Armémuseum/The Swedish Army Museum)

Nagant receivers which were modified in 1984 by Valmet and assembled in 1984–85 by the Finnish Defence Force Arsenal No. 1. New barrels were fitted in conjunction with the old receivers; and the Tkiv 85 is chambered for the Finnish 7.62×53mmR cartridge. Optics for sniper work include telescopic sights and night scopes.

THE MOSIN-NAGANT IN THE GREAT PATRIOTIC WAR

Owing to shortages of weapons, Red Army recruits were not issued rifles until action was imminent:

> Only the officers were given handguns, usually Nagan [*sic*] revolvers, a design that dated from the 1890s. It was an officer's exclusive privilege, too, to get an army wristwatch. Private soldiers got the bags and holsters, but much of the time they got nothing to put in them. Their tally of assorted empty luggage included a field bag, a bag for carrying biscuits, a strap for fastening their overcoat, a woollen flask cover, a bag for the things they had brought from home, a rifle sling, cartridge boxes and a cartridge belt. The weapons themselves, and even the ammunition rounds, were so precious that most men did not handle them until they took part in a field operation. But they were issued with an army token, the proof of their new status, and a small kettle. The things that had a personal use were the most treasured. 'Frontline soldiers would sometimes throw away their heavy rifles,' wrote one veteran, Gabriel Temkin. 'But never their spoons.' (Merridale 2005: 56)

The political officer – known as a *politruk* – played a key role in weapons training:

> The range of topics that they taught was wide indeed. *Politruks* were present at classes in target shooting, drill practice and rifle disassembly. They were the individuals who typed up individual scores, noting how

A Red Army instructor demonstrates the working of the bolt of the M1891 rifle to a group of young recruits who have yet to receive their uniforms and who still retain their civilian clothes. The bayonets are fixed in the ready position on their rifles, as per long-standing Russian military doctrine. The instructor´s rank badges are indistinct but he appears to be a junior platoon commander. (Courtesy of the Central Museum of the Armed Forces, Moscow via Stavka)

many men were 'excellent' in any field and inventing excuses for the many who were not ... With ideology so prominent in the men's timetable each day, extra hours had to be found to accommodate conventional forms of training. In 1939, the 'study day' was ten hours long; from March 1940, following the Finnish disaster, it was increased to twelve ... In fact, the only skills that most recruits had time to learn were very basic ones ... political meddling constantly undermined their confidence, and lack of time restricted the skills that they were able to learn. (Merridale 2005: 63–64, 68)

One of the more unusual uses of the M1891/30 rifle was as a 'handle' for a mine-detector head. The detector head slipped over the muzzle, allowing the soldier to continue to fire his rifle if needed. Here a soldier wearing *ushanka* headgear concentrates on the signals from his detector as he screens a patch of snow which may conceal a mine. Snow made mine detection very difficult as it obscured all tell-tale traces of disturbed ground. (Nik Cornish at www.stavka.org.uk)

Although rather long in the tooth, the Mosin-Nagant rifle appears to have remained popular despite its scarcity:

The rifle in question, at this stage, was a magazine-fed bolt-action model with a bayonet. Its design dated from the 1890s, but it was reliable and trusted by the men. The problem was that even when the factories in Tula and Izhevsk stepped up production after 1937, there were not enough guns available for every recruit to handle. Spare parts were another problem everywhere. The men who faced the Finns in 1939 had often trained for weeks with wooden replicas; enough, perhaps, to learn some drill, to try the handling when lying down or kneeling in a trench, but hopeless when it came to taking aim, to testing weight or balance in your hand ... Not surprisingly, reports from military camps painted a dismal picture of

A Degtyaryev DP-27 light-machine-gun team in action amid the ruins of a building. The assistant gunner is armed with an M1938 carbine for personal protection, to supplement the fire of the DP-27 and to offer some continuation while changing magazines or clearing jams. Both men wear M1940 steel helmets and woollen tunics. (From the fonds of the RGAKFD in Krasnogorsk via Stavka)

training and its effects. Large numbers of recruits, both officers and men, regularly failed to meet expected standards of rifle competence. Accidents, too, were alarmingly frequent. Even during daytime training there were instances of soldiers firing randomly when they were drunk. (Merridale 2005: 68–69)

When properly equipped, motivated and led, Stalin's infantrymen were formidable in the eyes of their German opponents:

The Germans genuinely feared Soviet bayonets, and troops were encouraged to use them for that reason. The problem, for many, was that they had no other choice. That June [1941], soldiers in Belorussia and Ukraine ran out of cartridges and bullets. Anastas Mikoyan recalled his government's surprise when it learned that the army had run out of rifles, too. 'We thought we surely had enough for the whole army,' he wrote in his memoir. 'But it turned out that a portion of our divisions had been assembled according to peacetime norms. Divisions that had been equipped with adequate numbers of rifles for wartime conditions held on to them, but they were all close to the front. When the Germans crossed the frontier and began to advance, these weapons ended up in the territory they controlled or else the Germans simply captured them. As a result, reservists going to the front ended up with no rifles at all.' (Merridale 2005: 124–25)

Militia (*opolchenie*) forces were rapidly absorbed into the Red Army, as witnessed by the experiences of A.E. Gordon: 'In the presence of members

As was the case in World War I, the Germans captured huge quantities of Mosin-Nagants from the Soviets during the Great Patriotic War. They were issued to rear-echelon troops to free up production of Mauser Kar 98k rifles for the front. (Tom Laemlein / Armor Plate Press)

of his local Communist Party branch, he and his friends took the Red Army oath and exchanged their black uniforms for the infantry's olive green. By then, he estimated, most of them had scarcely handled a real gun. Gordon had fired a training rifle twice' (Merridale 2005: 158).

SOVIET MOSIN-NAGANT SNIPING RIFLES

There is no evidence that the Russians deployed any snipers during World War I and no contemporary M1891 rifle fitted with a telescopic sight is known to exist. Once the Soviet Union had established itself in the years after the war, its military began to address this deficiency. It has to be remembered, however, that although it was Stalin's aim to rearm and re-equip the Red Army in a series of Five-Year Plans, finances were tight; the Army was desperately under-funded and such specialized equipment was not afforded

World War II production challenges

When Germany invaded the Soviet Union on 22 June 1941, the Soviets were ill-prepared for a major war. A lack of finances and economic resources coupled with Stalin's purge of senior officers in 1937, had left the Red Army ill-equipped, badly trained and without effective leadership – a state of affairs that was readily apparent from the Red Army's lamentable performance during the Winter War against Finland in 1939–40. Amazingly, another purge was instigated in the early month of the Great Patriotic War. This purge affected both the People's Commission for Armaments and that for Ammunition.

In 1939, the Tula Arsenal had stopped production of Mosin-Nagants altogether, having received instructions to concentrate on the poorly designed 7.62×54mmR Model 1938 Tokarev (or SVT-38) automatic rifle. This switch doubtless contributed to the poor production level of Mosin-Nagants early in the Great Patriotic War. German territorial gains were so rapid that Tula was threatened, so the plant was closed and its machinery moved to safety in the Ural Mountains. From that point the Izhevsk Arsenal became the Soviets' principal small-arms factory for the rest of the war. Sestroryetsk Arsenal suffered the same fate as Tula in the summer of 1941, with the approach of Finnish and (later) German troops. The plant and personnel were relocated to Leningrad where, under the banner of The Red Toolmaker factory, they manufactured sub-machine guns and other arms.

Production figures of M1891/30 rifles 1930–45

1930	102,000	1938	1,124,464
1931	154,000	1939	1,396,667
1932	283,451	1940	1,375,822
1933	239,290	1941	873,391
1934	300,590	1942	3,026,000
1935	136,959	1943	3,400,000
1936	not known	1944	not known
1937	560,545	1945	not known

Despite the rapid increase in production during wartime, these figures appear to be woefully inadequate given that the Red Army numbered over 6.8 million soldiers. In spite of this, the Mosin-Nagant M1891/30 was the most-produced bolt-action infantry rifle during World War II. The author Terence Lapin puts total production of the M1891/30 during the Great Patriotic War at 17,465,000 (Lapin 2003).

a high priority. Consequently, progress was slow. The modernization of the M1891 rifle in the late 1920s probably initiated the process, although Soviet industry had been producing good optical sights based on the designs of Emil Busch and Zeiss-Jena. Individual M1891/30s – specially selected for their accuracy – were taken off the production line and fitted with telescopic sights for sniper use made by Gustloff-Werke of Berlin.

By 1932, the Soviets had finalized the design of the sniping rifle which was subsequently designated '7.62 Milimetrya Vintovka Mosina snayperskaya' ('7.62 millimetre Mosin sniper's rifle'). The first Soviet telescopic sights were the 4× PE (Unified Model) which had an over-bore, split-ring mount; a graticule adjustable for windage and elevation; and a sight which incorporated a focus-adjustment sleeve. The sniping rifle itself

was fitted with a special bolt which had a purpose-made turned-down handle to prevent it fouling the sight when opened. Towards the end of the 1930s, the PE sight's design was improved, the new model being designated the PEM (Unified Model Modernized).

The Spanish Civil War proved to be an ideal testing ground for the new sniping rifle significant numbers of PE-sighted examples of which were sold by the Soviets to the Republicans. It took time for the rifles to be used effectively as the Spanish had no history either of hunting with rifles or of target marksmanship. This skill developed, however, as is illustrated by the following quotation from B. Lukin's 1938 book *Snipers in Modern Warfare*:

> The sniper positions worked very well. In December 1937, the positions of the Ninth Brigade located on the front to the north of Huesca killed 150 fascists in two weeks. Similar positions were set up by another brigade on the river Ebro. Here the line of Republican trenches was 500 metres away … shooting over that distance the snipers were able to put 5–6 insurgents out of action every day. (Quoted in Pegler 2004:160)

An M1891/30 sniping rifle fitted with a 3.5× PE (Unified Model) telescopic sight. Note the turned-down bolt handle, characteristic of all Soviet sniping rifles. The chequered focus-adjusting ring is at the rear. Elevation and windage are controlled by the screws in the two turrets. The mount was screwed – and sometimes silver soldered as well – onto the receiver of an M1891/30 rifle which had been specially selected for its accuracy. The PE sight mount had holes through its centre to allow the rifle's iron sights to be used in emergencies. (NRA Museums, NRAMuseums.com)

The Spanish Civil War proved to be an invaluable experience for the Soviets, who learned much about the art of sniping from the Republicans' effective deployment of snipers. The tactical importance of snipers in both attack and defence would form an important part of Soviet military doctrine in the subsequent Great Patriotic War.

In late 1942, the simpler and much smaller PU sight was introduced. This was a 3.5× telescope weighing 255g and featuring a three-post reticule adjustable for both windage and elevation, sighted to a maximum of 1,300m. It was mounted on a one-piece, over-bore mount secured by a large, easily removable screw. Although the PU sight was cheap and easy to manufacture, its sight mount was not adjustable for eye relief, which led to problems for some soldiers whose physiology did not suit the PU's dimensions. Nevertheless, the PU-sighted M1891/30 became the standard Soviet sniper rifle during the Great Patriotic War. During the war over 400,000 Soviet soldiers received basic sniper training; and once on the front line at Stalingrad, the training continued:

Female soldiers from a Red Army women's battalion march past carrying their M1891/30 rifles. Unusually for Soviet soldiers, they do not have their bayonets fixed or carried reversed on their rifles, possibly because no bayonets had been issued or because they are carried in scabbards obscured from view. Several Soviet female snipers are easily discernible by virtue of the canvas covers over the telescopic sight on their *snayperskaya* sniper rifles. Their greatcoats/blankets/shelter sections are worn Russian style, *en banderole*. The M1891/30 was a lengthy rifle, which caused problems for the sniper when it was slung. The celebrated sniper Vasily Grigoryevich Zaitsev noted that 'The long rifle on your back is constantly shifting from side to side, forcing you to stop and adjust its position' (Zaitsev 2009: 82). (Courtesy of the Central Museum of the Armed Forces, Moscow via Stavka)

... the Lazur Chemical Plant remained in Soviet hands. In one section of the block-long building, Russian instructors now conducted an intensive course in sharpshooting. Against the wall of a long room, they painted helmets, observation slits, and outlines of human torsos. At the other end, they stood over trainees and coached them on sniper techniques. All day long, the plant echoed to rifle fire from within as the recruits practiced shooting at the targets. Those who graduated from this impromptu school went immediately to the edge of no-man's-land where they began to take a fearful toll of the enemy. (Craig 2015)

The Soviet sniper's primary objectives were threefold. First, the sniper was to undertake counter-sniping work to destroy any assets that could disrupt the advance of their own troops. Second, the sniper was to destroy the enemy command structure by killing commanders at all levels. Third, the sniper was to destroy enemy soldiers conducting or adjusting fire, such as artillery forward observers. In terms of ammunition use, Soviet snipers chose the most appropriate round available to them that would destroy the target, whether that be ball, heavy-ball, armour-piercing, incendiary or explosive.

This Hungarian-made Mosin-Nagant M1891/30 rifle fitted with a PU telescopic sight was captured from a North Vietnamese Army sniper in 1970 and subsequently presented to the NRA Museum by the CO of Detachment C3, Army of the Republic of Vietnam Special Forces, Colonel Nguyen Thanh Chuan. This serves to illustrate the wide dispersal of Soviet-inspired military small arms throughout the Communist world. Hungarian-made Mosin-Nagant rifles exhibit a better quality of wood and a superior metal finish than their Soviet-made counterparts. (NRA Museums, NRAMuseums.com)

MOSIN-NAGANT ACCESSORIES

Bayonets

The bayonet, known as a *shtik* in Russian, was a socket type with a quatrefoil ground blade and a flattened, 'screwdriver' point. Russia was the last major power to issue a socket-bayonet for its rifles; and the adoption of an old-fashioned socket-bayonet at a time when most other powers were looking to knife-bayonets serves to emphasize the essentially conservative nature of the Russian military. No scabbard was issued, as Russian military doctrine required the bayonet to be affixed to the rifle at all times. The Germans, Austrians and Finns recognized the impracticability of this and issued leather or rolled sheet-steel scabbards for captured bayonets.

The original M1891 bayonet had a locking ring which slipped over the front sight and then turned to the right to secure it on the barrel. There are several different slots which give the blade a different orientation to the muzzle when the blade is fixed. Those bayonets made in Wiener-Neustadt for M1891 rifles captured by the Austrians have straight slots in their sockets. Sometime in 1915, an experimental bayonet designed by E.K. Kabakov was issued in small numbers. This was no more than the blade of a Berdan II bayonet welded to a simplified socket. It was not manufactured in great numbers, however, and suffered from being 44g heavier than the standard M1891 bayonet. While this does not seem a massive increase in weight, it would alter the bullet's mean point of impact while shooting with the bayonet fixed. When the Soviets modernized the Mosin-Nagant rifle in the 1930s, the rotating locking ring was replaced by a spring-loaded button catch with a chequered head to make the bayonet easier to fix or detach.

Neither the M1908 carbine nor the M1938 carbine took a bayonet. The M1944 carbine had a permanently attached folding spike-bayonet, however, mounted on the right side of the barrel. It swung out and was locked in place by a spring-loaded collar. The Russians had dabbled with folding bayonets since at least 1912, when the experimental Kholodovskii bayonet was trialled, and from 1942 to 1948 a further five different types of folding bayonet were subjected to tests. Loss of the folding bayonet was prevented because it was permanently attached to the rifle or carbine and was secure in both the battle and march positions.

Barbed-wire-cutting devices

During World War I, as fluid warfare stagnated and combatants on all sides dug in behind barbed-wire entanglements, there was a need to give the individual infantryman the means by which to cut the wire. Conventional cutters were issued, but these were cumbersome and needed both hands to use, making them of limited use in a fast-moving tactical situation. Devices properly known as wire-breakers were developed which trapped individual strands of wire over the rifle's muzzle so that a bullet cut the wire when it was fired. These devices could be kept permanently attached and did not interfere with the use of the rifle or bayonet. They also had the advantage that the rifle did not have to be put down while the wire was being cut. Some such devices relied on

the rifle being used as a lever to facilitate the cut as the wire was pushed into two small blades in the angle of a pair of spring-loaded jaws. The Russians also issued a wire-breaker with a forked end that channelled the wire across the muzzle in readiness for the bullet to cut it.

The scale of issue of these devices is unknown and extant specimens are very rare today, mainly in excavated condition. The advantages of the rifle-mounted cutter or breaker were mainly theoretical, however, and their use did not continue into the Soviet era.

Grenade-launching cups

During World War I, after the US Government purchased large numbers of M1891s from Remington and New England Westinghouse, it is reported that experimental Vivien-Bessières grenade-launching cups were produced in small numbers. This is entirely logical as other US service rifles had VB grenade-launchers at the time. Perhaps this initial development was not pursued as the United States did not issue M1891s to its American Expeditionary Force troops on the Western Front.

Pederson devices

Very small numbers of the Pederson self-loading 'pistol' device are known to have been made for M1891s, in an attempt to convert them to assault rifles capable of self-loading fire.

BraMit sound moderators

In certain military situations it is desirable to use a firearm fitted with a device to reduce its sound signature on discharge. A sound moderator is at its most effective when used with subsonic ammunition; that is, ammunition with projectiles travelling at less than 340m/sec at sea level. It will not reduce the sound of the sonic boom of the bullet, but it will make it appear non-directional, disguising the location from which it was fired. A moderator also quietens muzzle-blast by slowing down the escaping gases as they leave the muzzle. As the Mosin-Nagant cartridge was a powerful round, discharging its bullet at a velocity of about 730m/sec, it was difficult to reduce its sound on firing.

Effective sound moderators for firearms had been developed as early as 1908 by Hiram P. Maxim, son of Sir Hiram S. Maxim, the inventor of the machine gun. During the 1930s, the Soviet Union experimented with sound moderators for military firearms. None of the trials was successful as the moderators not only failed to reduce the rifle's noise on firing, but also affected its accuracy. It was not until June 1940 that the Mitny brothers produced a really effective sound moderator which used its own specially downloaded ammunition. Their design, known as the 'BraMit' (the name derives from Brat'ya Mitny; Brothers Mitny), had two expansion chambers and two rubber plugs pierced to allow the bullets to exit. A standard bayonet fitting was used to attach the device to the barrel.

BraMit sound moderators were made by the Tula, Mednogorsk and Podolsk arms-production plants. Production totals are unknown, but probably exceeded 50,000. Surviving specimens are very rare. The BraMit was issued to snipers and to NKVD (People's Commissariat for Internal Affairs) troops. It was also favoured by partisans, who found it very useful for guerrilla warfare. Both the Finns and the Germans used captured BraMits. Under the umbrella of *Fremdengeräte* (foreign devices/equipments), the Germans designated the device Schalldämpfer Nr. 254(r).

Cartridges intended for use with the BraMit sound moderator were loaded with a reduced charge to produce subsonic velocities. They were distinguished either by black-painted bullets or by the heads of the cases being varnished green. There were initially two types of rubber plug for warm or cold weather. Later, Lend-Lease aviation rubber was used, which was suitable for all temperatures.

ABOVE Bayonets for Russian Mosin-Nagant rifles. Above is a Soviet M1891/30 bayonet; below are an Imperial M1891 bayonet and its scabbard (believed to be Austro-Hungarian from World War I). (Author's Collection)

ABOVE An interesting rear view of a group of Russian Civil War-era troops. Unusually, they carry their M1891 rifles without bayonets on them, either fixed or reversed. The nearest man's bayonet socket can just be seen on his left-hand side, apparently carried in a scabbard. Two methods of attaching the rifle sling are also evident. These men wear the excellent winter *papaha* astrakhan fur hats and appear to be wearing captured German M1895 *Tornister* backpacks with loops for mess-tin straps. (Nik Cornish at www.stavka.org.uk)

The author firing a Finnish 7.62mm M/39 rifle on an impromptu rifle range in Suffolk, UK. (Author's Collection)

The Soviet Union lauded its most successful snipers as a conscious propaganda contribution to the war effort. For example, in 1943 Lyudmilla Mykhailivna Pavlichenko (309 confirmed kills) was honoured by her image – firing an M1891/30 sniper rifle – appearing on a postage stamp. Many Red Army snipers were decorated, some being made Heroes/Heroines of the Soviet Union.

Production figures for Mosin-Nagant sniping rifles are not known, but they must have been considerable given the importance the Soviets attached to snipers, with some 54,000 PE scopes supplied from 1932 to 1938 alone. What is beyond doubt is the fact that the M1891/30 sniper rifle was a very important weapon in the Soviet arsenal.

THE MOSIN-NAGANT AFTER 1945

In the late 1950s, the Soviet Union converted many of its M1891/30 rifles into M1938 or M1944 carbines. The last M1891/30 sniping rifles were issued in about 1968. Poland manufactured Mosin-Nagant rifles and carbines under licence; some of the M1944s are dated from the early 1950s. Hungary produced very good-quality M1891/30 rifles and M1944 carbines, these weapons being distinguished by the digits '02' marked on their major components. During the early 1950s Romania relegated many serviceable M1891/30 rifles to war-reserve status. These have red painted bands on their stocks and are marked *Insructie*. Unserviceable rifles were rendered incapable of being fired by having their strikers shortened and being marked as *Exercitu* with black-painted stocks.

USING THE MOSIN-NAGANT

Loading and firing

Before firing any Mosin-Nagant rifle or carbine, it is as well to have it checked over by a competent gunsmith who can attest to its material soundness and safety to use. Wipe any excess oil or storage grease from the bore; the patch should emerge clean and dry once all the oil has been wiped out.

Ammunition for Mosin-Nagant rifles is cheap and plentiful. Ex-Soviet ammunition (packed in 440-round 'sardine' cans) is readily available; but most such ammunition is steel cased and Berdan primed, and it cannot be reloaded easily. Many of today's ammunition companies load the 7.62×54mmR cartridge, but their ammunition is more expensive. Modern

This sequence of photographs shows the loading of an M1891/30 sniping rifle with its telescopic sight removed. The bolt is closed (**1**). The bolt is opened and a charger of five cartridges is inserted into the charger guide (**2**). The cartridges are pushed into the magazine with the thumb (**3**). The charger is removed with forefinger and thumb (**4**), ready to chamber the first cartridge as the bolt closes. (Author's Collection)

commercial cartridges are made with Boxer-primed brass cases which may be reloaded. If the rifle is to be used to hunt, ethical practice demands that cartridges loaded with soft- or hollow-point bullets be used.

Loading practice with dummy cartridges prior to shooting live ammunition is always a good idea as it leads to confidence in handling the rifle. 'Dummy' cartridges are easily made by pulling the bullets from live rounds with an inertia bullet-puller, emptying out the propellant and striking the primers. Small holes (about 2.5mm in diameter) should be drilled in the case wall. The empty bullets can then be reinserted. If the struck cap is removed from the primer pocket, this can be painted red so as to remove any doubt that this is not a live cartridge. The insertion of a shotgun pellet or small ball-bearing into the case before reseating the bullet is another very useful audible indicator for a dummy round.

Owing to the interrupter in the magazine, the Mosin-Nagant can easily be loaded with single cartridges. However, a charger of five makes loading much easier. To load with a charger, press it into the charger guide until it stops. Then, with your little finger, lift up cartridges two to five while pressing the whole stack down with your thumb. All the cartridges will be loaded into the magazine in one go. Pull the charger out of the guides and push the bolt forwards to chamber the first cartridge. (Unlike the Mauser series of rifles, the charger has to be removed by hand and does not fall away when the bolt is worked.)

The safety is awkward, and its application and disengagement should be rehearsed by dry runs on an empty chamber or dummy cartridge until the

59

This pair of photographs shows (left) an M1891/30 sniping rifle, action cocked, ready to fire, and (right) the same weapon with safety catch applied and cocking piece locked on the left side of the receiver. (Author's Collection)

technique for using it is mastered. To apply the safety, grasp the bolt-cocking piece in your right hand. Pull the cocking piece back slightly and turn the bolt anticlockwise through about 30 degrees. The cocking piece latches onto the left rear of the receiver and the rifle cannot be fired as the cocking piece and firing pin are now locked in place. To disengage the safety, pull back on the cocking piece again, turn the bolt clockwise and allow the cocking piece to run forwards until the sear engages. The rifle is now ready to fire.

After firing with ex-Soviet military-surplus ammunition, it is essential to wipe the bore thoroughly with an ammonia-based household cleaner to neutralize the corrosive residue from the Soviet mercuric primers. Modern ammunition is far less corrosive, but careful cleaning is always needed. The bore should also be wiped out with a proprietary bore solvent and preserved for storage with light machine oil.

A modern cleaning pull-through or purpose-made rod is the best option. If cleaning from the muzzle with the rifle's own cleaning rod, always use the rod guide to protect the muzzle crown. Steel parts should be wiped with an oily rag. The stock can be cleaned with a wet cloth soaked in warm water. Rifles are best stored with their butts uppermost so that the oil does not drain onto the stock. This is important because mineral oil has a detrimental effect on wood fibres.

Cleaning

For all that Mosin-Nagants are 'no-frills' rifles of almost agricultural construction and simplicity, they have remarkably sophisticated cleaning kits. The barrel is cleaned with the under-barrel rod, which has a tubular collar slipped over the bottom on the end. The short drift becomes a tommy bar which passes through the holes to form a gripping handle. In order to protect the muzzle crown when cleaning, the muzzle protector provides a central hole to guide the rod. The rod is pushed through the hole before the jag or brush is screwed on. The jag or brush can be tightened by using the large notch on the screwdriver which engages with flats machined onto these items.

The bore is first brushed out and then swabbed with oakum, hemp or tow soaked in solvent. An official poster showed this material wrapped

around the jag in a figure of eight. When the cleaning material runs out clean, the bore is oiled.

The Russians clearly intended that the soldier should dismantle the bolt completely for cleaning, which is why the screwdriver had notches to indicate correct firing-pin protrusion when the bolt was reassembled. The screwdrivers are often marked with the numerals '75' and '95' by way of indicating the protrusion depths. The striker should touch the '75' mark but should not exceed the '95' mark.

Russian unit armourers working on M1891 rifles in an improvised field workshop (note the rack of M1891s to the left of the picture). The sophisticated nature of the cleaning kit and its accompanying combination tool made the Russian soldier as self-sufficient as possible when it came to regular maintenance and cleaning of his rifle. Only serious repairs would need to be referred to unit technical personnel or a base workshop. (Nik Cornish at www. stavka.org.uk)

A typical cleaning kit for Mosin-Nagants, including canvas pouch with tape closer, stamped-steel combination tool, oil/alkali solution bottle, rod collar, brush, jag, muzzle guide and tommy bar. The combination tool could be seen with a wide variety of markings. Sometimes a screwdriver with a wooden handle and a reversible blade was issued. All the tools are contained in a cloth pouch with a simple tape closure to the flap. (Author's Collection)

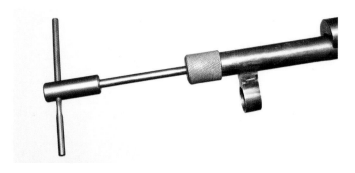

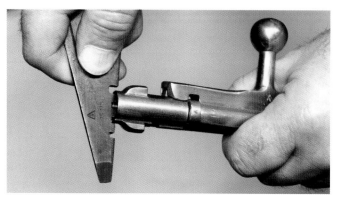

The bolt-connector bar was designed to be used as a spanner on the striker shank when adjusting firing-pin protrusion. Screwdrivers had reversible blades of different widths and were made with both squared and rounded wooden handles. Some rare specimens were made from knurled steel tubing and contained part of the cleaning kit as well as doubling as a handle for the rod. These examples appear to be restricted to the 1930s and the early years of the Great Patriotic War. Later examples were made from stamped steel sheet with a large teardrop-shaped cut-out. This cut-out was to save steel while maintaining strength and did not function as a wrench or other type of implement. These later screwdrivers are often

ABOVE Cleaning tools in use. Here, the rod collar, muzzle guide and tommy bar are assembled and fitted to the rod; inserted ready for cleaning into the muzzle of an M1891/30 sniping rifle. (Author's Collection)

BELOW The combination tool in use. Here, the notches on the combination tool are used to check that the depth of the striker protrusion is correct. The large notch is a wrench for the striker. (Author's Collection)

marked with an arsenal stamp denoting where they were made. Larger, but simpler, versions of the screwdriver had only the notch for unscrewing the firing pin or tightening tools onto the rod.

Mosin-Nagants not in regular use were to be cleaned not less than once every seven days. Otherwise they were to be cleaned after guard duty or training, especially if blank cartridges had been used. After field firing on a range the bore and bolt head were to be cleaned and oiled immediately on the range and then the rest of the rifle thoroughly cleaned upon return to barracks. The rifle was to be checked for corrosion daily over the next three or four days. In combat or prolonged field exercises the rifle was to be cleaned daily, taking advantage of lulls in battle or exercise.

In winter, Lubricant No. 21, a thick, light-yellow grease-like petroleum jelly, was used to counteract low temperatures which led to jams and caused oils to freeze. A variety of alkaline solvents were issued, depending on the availability of the ingredients needed to make them. Their essential property was that they neutralized the acid engendered by the combustion of the propellant, which caused rust in the bore.

OIL BOTTLES

The Mosin-Nagant oil bottle, of which there are three main variations, is one of the most distinctive items of military rifle equipment. There is an inevitable crossover between those oil bottles intended for the Mosin-Nagants, the SKS-45 self-loading carbine and the AK-47 assault rifle. Most oil bottles are made from tin-plate and have screw-caps.

Round, single spout

This is the original type of oil bottle. Those issued in Tsarist Russia had the Romanov eagle stamped on one side and the Cyrillic letters over an arrow on the other. These oil bottles are seldom encountered. The Soviets copied them and early examples are known with the hammer and sickle on one side. Three other later examples are stamped either with discs on both sides, a large circle on one side, or the arrow with a triangular Izhevsk Arsenal mark.

Round, twin cell and double spout

These are from the later Soviet/Warsaw Pact era. One side has the Cyrillic character **H** for the letter 'N' (Oil in Russian is *nyeft*.) The other is the Cyrillic character **Щ** for 'Tsch' (*Tschelochnoy sostav* is Russian for an alkaline solvent to deal with corrosive primer residue). The Chinese issued the same type of oil bottles with the characters for 'oil' and 'salt' on the front.

Cuboid, twin cell and double spout

Again, these are from the later Soviet/Warsaw Pact era. One side has the Cyrillic character for oil and the other the character for alkaline solvent. The Chinese also issued them with the characters for 'oil' and 'salt' on the front. The Poles painted one of the sides red. Most types are of heavy construction, but one type exists made from much lighter-gauge tin-plate with much squarer end-edges.

Other oil bottles

Another type of round twin-cell oil bottle in brass is known. It is very crudely soldered down a central seam and its basic construction suggests wartime production. A slightly smaller and better-quality oil bottle in brass with knurled caps is marked with the Cyrillic letters spelling 'LOD' and 'CEESH'. The final type of oil bottle likely to be encountered was clearly a wartime emergency issue as it is simply two small, screw-cap tins – similar to those used for paint or polish – joined together at their bases. These oil bottles are marked with the Cyrillic letter for 'N' and 'Tsch' respectively. During sieges or in circumstances when troops had to be supplied with locally procured substitute items, it would make sense to use a serviceable container already in civilian production.

Finnish oil bottles and cleaning kits

The Finns issued tools and cleaning kits of exactly the same types as the Russians. The Finnish oil bottle was a smaller version of the round single-spout type, with the 'SA' (Suomen Armeija; Finnish Army) or 'SkY' (Suojeluskuntain Yliesikunta; Finnish Civil Guard General HQ) mark on both sides. They were made by G.W. Sohlberg Ab Oy and marked on the cap accordingly. The Finnish Civil Guard issued an elliptical-section oil bottle marked 'SkY' and often painted olive green.

Finnish cleaning-kit bags are much larger than Russian ones and are held shut by tying two tapes in a bow. They can be found with both 'SA' and 'SkY' markings. Members of the *Lotta Svärd* (the women's auxiliary of the Civil Guard) also made bags for the military from any available suitable fabric.

ABOVE Representative oil bottles for Mosin-Nagant rifles. In the top row are four examples of the cuboid style with twin cells for oil and an alkali cleaning solution (L to R: Romanian, Hungarian, Chinese and Soviet). In the middle row are four examples of the round style with single spout (L to R: Bulgarian, Romanian, Soviet (Izhevsk Arsenal) and Finnish). In the bottom row are four examples of the round twin-cell style (L to R: Soviet (emergency issue made from two small tins), Chinese, crude brass (Romanian?) and Soviet). (Author's Collection)

IMPACT
A long-lived weapon

ASSESSING THE MOSIN-NAGANT

Some idea of the effectiveness of the M1891 rifle can be gained by comparing its attributes to those of contemporary rifles adapted by major powers around the same time. In doing so, however, it is important to compare like with like. As a general principle, most powers adopted reduced-calibre (6.5–8mm) repeating rifles firing smokeless cartridges in the later years of the 1880s or the early years of the 1890s. As the Mosin-Nagant was adopted by Imperial Russia in 1891, any comparisons made to assess its impact must select rifles from around that year – it would be pointless to compare the M1891 with the improved rifles issued from the late 1890s up to the decade preceding World War I. By way of illustration, the United Kingdom first issued its legendary .303in Short Magazine Lee-Enfield (SMLE) bolt-action rifle in 1905. Most commentators agree that this was an excellent rifle: it was for universal issue, was short and handy, and had a ten-shot-capacity detachable magazine which could be loaded with two five-round chargers of cartridges very easily. Even so, it was only an improved version of the .303in Lee-Metford Mk I, first adopted in 1888. If the comparisons are to have any meaning, then earlier rifles must be chosen. Equally, the ballistics of the early round-nosed rather than later 'spitzer' bullets must be used.

The rifles chosen for the comparison are: the 8mm Mannlicher M1886/90 (Austria-Hungary); the 8mm Mauser-Mannlicher M1888 (Germany); the .303 Lee-Metford Mk I of 1888 (United Kingdom); the 6.5mm Mannlicher-Carcano M1891 (Italy); the 7mm Mauser M1892 (Spain); and the .30-40 Krag-Jørgensen M1892 (United States). The date spread has been limited to three years before 1891, the year 1891 itself and one year thereafter. By way of a long-stop comparison, the French 8mm Lebel M1886 has also been included, as it was the world's first reduced-calibre repeating rifle firing a cartridge loaded with smokeless propellant to be adopted.

Handiness and durability

It should be remembered that in the late 1880s, infantry were believed to need a long rifle with a long bayonet to defend themselves against cavalry. In an era of long rifle and long bayonet, however, the Mosin-Nagant was longer than the average, which made it unbalanced and not very handy to use. As for weight: at about 4kg, the Mosin-Nagant was typical for a service rifle of the period.

The bolt of the 8mm Mannlicher M1886/90 relied on a rising wedge to lock it. (Although in theory a straight-pull bolt can be operated a lot quicker than a turn-bolt, it is tiring to do so.) The action was comparatively weak with no locking lugs on the bolt head; the rifle was also complicated to make. The 8mm Mauser-Mannlicher M1888 was not particularly strong as it had a split receiver. It was also complex to manufacture, with a separate head. It had an excellent flag safety on the rear of the bolt.

Although it did not have a particularly strong action, the .303 Lee-Metford Mk I was very quick to operate – it cocked on closing, which

Imperial Russian soldiers armed with early versions of the M1891 rifle. These rifles do not have the sling slots and are fitted with conventional swivels. The M1891 waist-belt ammunition pouches are complemented by cotton bandoliers. (Courtesy of the Central Museum of the Armed Forces, Moscow via Stavka)

Rifle	Overall length*	Weight**
8mm Mannlicher M1886/90	152cm	4.04kg
8mm Mauser-Mannlicher M1888	170cm†	4.08kg
.303 Lee Metford Mk I of 1888	155cm	4.31kg
6.5mm Mannlicher-Carcano M1891	158cm	3.86kg
7mm Mauser M1892	149cm	3.97kg
.30-40 Krag-Jørgensen M1892	155cm	4.08kg
8mm Lebel M1886	183cm	4.08kg
7.62mm Mosin-Nagant M1891	178cm	4.08kg

* Rounded to the nearest centimetre, with bayonet fixed.

** Unloaded weight. Actual weights between individual rifles of the same model may vary due to timber density.

† The M71 bayonet has a 46cm blade; the M1888 rifle could be used with shorter bayonet types.

accelerated the rate of fire – and could be fired without the shooter raising his head. It had an excellent safety catch that could be engaged with the thumb alone, and was not particularly complicated to build. By contrast, the 6.5mm Mannlicher-Carcano M1891 was a modified Mauser action that was complicated to make and had an awkwardly positioned safety.

The 7mm Mauser Model 1892 had a strong action that would evolve into the 98 action – the strongest known, with its three locking lugs on the bolt and solid receiver bridge. Complicated to make, the Mauser Model 1892 had an excellent flag safety on the rear of the bolt. The .30-40 Krag-Jørgensen M1892 has one of the smoothest bolt actions known. It was not a very strong rifle, however, and was very complicated to make. Like the Mauser, it had an excellent flag safety on the rear of the bolt. The 8mm Lebel M1886 was very complicated to make, but it had no safety.

Technologically, the Mosin-Nagant M1891 rifle is difficult to compare with other designs as it was unique. It had an almost agricultural crudeness about it yet it was strong and easy to make. Even though it had a complicated but very strong bolt, it could be easily dismantled into its component parts without the soldier needing to go to a field-repair workshop. The bolt aside, the rest of the rifle was easy to manufacture. The very effective safety was difficult to apply; it had to be pulled backwards against the force of the mainspring and then twisted so that the cocking piece locked off against the receiver wall.

Magazine capacity and ease of loading

The Mannlicher M1886/90 had a capacity of five cartridges; it used an en bloc clip making for rapid loading. The magazine could not be used without the clips, however, and could not be 'topped off' using single rounds. A bottle-necked cartridge, the 8mm Mannlicher proved to be unsuitable for large-capacity box magazines for automatic weapons.

As with the Mannlicher M1886/90, the Mauser-Mannlicher M1888 had a five-cartridge capacity and employed an en bloc clip; again, the magazine could not be used without the clips and could not be topped off using single rounds. The cartridge case was straight-walled, making it readily adaptable to box magazines and future automatic weapons.

The Lee-Metford Mk I had a capacity of eight cartridges (ten from 1893); it had no charger. Its detachable magazine, chained to the rifle, could be topped off using single rounds while keeping the bolt closed and a round in the chamber ready to fire. It was slow to fill. A bottle-necked cartridge, the .303 British would not at first blush prove readily adaptable to automatic weapons. However, the excellent .303in Bren light machine gun would get around this problem with its curved magazine.

The Mannlicher-Carcano M1891 shared many characteristics of the Mauser-Mannlicher M1888, but with a six-cartridge capacity. Spain's 7mm Mauser M1892 held five cartridges, and was loaded by stripper clip (charger). Very quick to use, it could be topped off using single rounds, but the bolt had to be kept open and the rifle was not immediately ready to fire. The straight-walled cartridge case was adaptable to box magazines and automatic weapons.

Soviet soldiers on patrol, *c.*1939. They all wear loose snow suits for camouflage. The leader carries an M1891/30 rifle with fixed bayonet. (Photo by Mark Redkin/ FotoSoyuz/Getty Images)

The Krag-Jørgensen M1892 had a five-cartridge capacity; these were poured into the magazine and there was no charger. The magazine could be topped off using single rounds whilst keeping the bolt closed and a round in the chamber ready to fire. It was slow to fill. The bottle-necked design of the .30-40 Krag cartridge was superseded by the .30-06, a modified Mauser design.

The Lebel M1886 had a Kropatschek-type tubular magazine holding eight cartridges with one on the lifter; it could be topped off using single rounds, but the bolt had to be kept open and the rifle was not immediately ready to fire. It was very slow to fill. The swollen, bottle-necked cartridge case was not adaptable to automatic weapons, as evidenced by the unreliability of the dreadful Chauchat machine rifle of World War I.

The Mosin-Nagant M1891 held five cartridges loaded by a charger. The interrupter meant that the magazine could be topped off using single rounds, but the bolt had to be kept open and the rifle was not immediately ready to fire. It was very quick to fire. In terms of magazine capacity and speed of loading, the M1891 was as good as the 7mm Mauser Model 1892, one of the most technologically advanced rifles of its time. In spite of its old-fashioned, bottle-necked design, the 7.62×54mmR cartridge proved infinitely adaptable to both belt and box magazine-fed automatic weapons, viz. the SVT-40 self-loading rifle, surviving into the 21st century. The Soviets were clearly so impressed with it that they designed the large pan magazine for using the round in the Degtyaryev light machine gun of 1928.

Power

In ballistic terms, 'power' is a somewhat clumsy and inaccurate term to use. If kinetic energy (measured at the muzzle) is designated as representing power, however, a useful comparative table can be compiled.

Rifle	Power*
8mm Mannlicher M1886/90	2,750 joules
8mm Mauser-Mannlicher M1888	2,980 joules
.303 Lee Metford Mk I of 1888	2,510 joules**
6.5mm Mannlicher-Carcano M1891	2,580 joules
7mm Mauser M1892	2,740 joules
.30-40 Krag-Jørgensen M1892	2,640 joules
8mm Lebel M1886	2,980 joules†
7.62mm Mosin-Nagant M1891	2,620 joules††

* All values are rounded to the nearest 10 joules.

** With the cordite Mk I cartridge, adopted November 1891.

† With the Balle M bullet.

†† With its original round-nosed bullet.

After it was improved with better bullets and propellants, the round used in the Mosin-Nagant M1891 developed about 3,660 joules and approximated to the excellent US .30-06 Springfield cartridge.

Summing up

The Mosin-Nagant was an overly long and ungainly rifle. It was easy to make, however, and the individual riflemen could undertake much of the day-to-day cleaning, maintenance and adjustment required of it. Its cartridge was exceptional when fully developed and would become the most long-lived military cartridge in the world. By comparison with other rifles, the Mosin-Nagant was not so deficient as to be obsolete even as it was introduced. It was robust and would function in poor conditions. Perhaps the fault lay not in the rifle itself, but in the inherently conservative Russian military that should have modernized it in the decade before World War I. The Soviet modernization in 1930 was a case of too little, too late.

REPLACING THE MOSIN-NAGANT

By the end of the Great Patriotic War, the Soviet rifleman armed with an M1891/30 rifle had declined in importance when compared to the submachine-gunner with a PPS-43 or PPSh-41. With their high rates of fire, submachine guns were much more useful in the urban close-combat situations that had come to dominate warfare. Besides which, submachine guns were cheap to build and did not require the accuracy of machining that a rifle did. As Soviet submachine guns fired the 7.62×25mm bottle-necked cartridge used in the Tokarev TT-33 pistol, rifle-producing plants could be used for producing submachine-gun barrels as rifles, the calibre being the same. It was found that a barrel blank for an M1891/30 rifle could be used to produce two submachine-gun barrels, thus giving economies of scale.

A World War II-era Soviet infantry section advances through ruined buildings. The soldier in the foreground fires his M1891/30 rifle in support of his comrades armed with PPS-43 and PPSh-41 submachine guns. By the last years of the Great Patriotic War, the submachine gun had become the Soviet infantry's signature weapon, with much less reliance being put on the Mosin-Nagant rifle. This photograph clearly shows the leather sling-retaining straps running through slots in the stock. Note that one soldier wears ankle-boots and puttees instead of the usual high leather boots. (Courtesy of the Central Museum of the Armed Forces, Moscow via Stavka)

In the late 1940s, the Soviet Union adopted the Simonov SKS-45 self-loading carbine with its intermediate 7.62×39mm cartridge. Following the brief interlude of the SKS-45, the stage was set for the full-scale implementation and adoption of the AK-47 Kalashnikov assault rifle.

TECHNICAL IMPACT

The Mosin-Nagant rifle made no meaningful technological impact on the weapon designers of the world when it was first introduced into Russian service in 1891. It was already obsolescent at the time it was issued and looked rather old-fashioned. It was a rifle that had no new features or aspects of design and which looked backwards rather than ahead to the new century. Its importance lies in the sheer numbers made – estimated at 37 million rifles and carbines. It was the Russian soldier's principal firearm for about 60 years, making it long-lived by any standards. As the Soviet Union extended its influence by promoting (or enforcing) Marxism/ Leninism ideology in Eastern Europe, so the Mosin-Nagant became the main infantry rifle of Soviet satellite countries.

It is remarkable that the basic design did not change from the last years of the 19th century to its twilight in the 1950s. The M1891 survived two world wars with only cosmetic modifications because it was 'soldier proof' and would function in the coldest of weathers. These two factors were vitally important to Russia which had a largely illiterate and unsophisticated peasant army that often found itself fighting in sub-zero temperatures.

Chinese and Czechoslovak Mosin-Nagants

Following its victory in the Great Patriotic War in 1945, the Soviet Union no longer had the urgent need to produce small arms for its own defence. The opportunity now presented itself to further the cause of world communism by giving military aid to other communist states, notably the People's Republic of China (PRC). The future lay with the assault rifle and the bolt-action Mosin-Nagant was now considered obsolete. Consequently,

the Soviet Union could afford to be generous towards its ideological ally in the East. Rather than sharing the technology of the self-loading Simonov or Kalashnikov systems, however, it gave the Chinese the machinery to build their own Mosin-Nagant M1944 carbines. This was an effective use of military aid: an ally was supported – albeit not with the very latest technology – and obsolete machinery cost little to give away.

These Chinese versions were designated Type 53 carbines by the PRC and were essentially Chinese-marked copies of the Soviet M1944 carbine. They were well-made arms, stocked in a shellac-finished Chinese wood called *chu*. Type 53 carbines with 1960s production dates are known; they are probably the last Mosin-Nagants ever made. Some Type 53 carbines have patriotic inscriptions in Chinese characters on their stocks.

As China burgeoned into a world power, it went through the same phases of rearmament as the Soviet Union, adopting its own version of the Simonov, the Type 56 carbine, in 1956. In turn, it passed on its obsolete military arms to Albania, Cambodia, North Vietnam, Yugoslavia and

The designer of the SKS lightweight self-loading carbine was Sergei Gavrilovich Simonov (1894–1986), who started his career as an arms technician during World War I, subsequently attending the Moscow Polytechnic before working at the Tula Arsenal under the celebrated Captain Vasili Federov. The SKS – the first Soviet firearm to fire an intermediate-size rifle cartridge – has a charger-loaded ten-round box magazine and a folding spike-bayonet. It was rendered obsolete within a few years of its adoption by the AK-47 Kalashnikov assault rifle. (NRA Museums, NRAMuseums.com)

A US Marine examines an abandoned North Vietnamese Army Type 53 carbine, large quantities of which were supplied to North Vietnam by the People's Republic of China during the Vietnam War. The spike-bayonet is deployed and the bolt is open. The survival of a bolt-action firearm in an era dominated by fully automatic assault rifles is remarkable and testament to the Mosin-Nagant's reliability and rugged nature. (Tom Laemlein / Armor Plate Press)

The Chinese Type 53 bolt-action carbine was a direct copy of its Soviet M1944 counterpart. The view from the right-hand side shows the carbine with its spike-bayonet folded against the stock when not in use; that from the left-hand side shows the bayonet in the fixed position. (NRA Museums, NRAMuseums.com)

numerous African states. As Chinese regular forces rearmed with the Type 56 assault rifle, the Type 53 carbines were given to the People's Militia for use in a purely defensive role. The North Vietnamese Army used many Type 53 carbines in the Vietnam War.

Chinese Type 53 carbines featured webbing slings like their Soviet counterparts, but they were flimsier and of a lighter shade of green. A green leatherette pouch for 20 rounds in chargers was also issued, the lids of which were kept closed by brown leather Y-shaped straps. Twin-cell Soviet-style oil/solvent bottles marked with Chinese characters completed the ancillary equipment.

In 1954, in response to the drive to harmonize all Warsaw Pact countries' weapons with those of the Soviet Union, Czechoslovakia adopted a sniping rifle, the vz.54, based on the Mosin-Nagant action. The vz.54 was only in production until 1958, by which time just over 5,400 units had been made. It was essentially a sporting-style rifle with a pistol-grip half-stock and a Czech-made heavy barrel for enhanced accuracy. It also had Mauser rifle features including front sight and hood, leaf rear sight and side-mounted sling-points. It used a unique 2.5× Meopta telescopic sight on a single-piece mount on the left-hand side of the action. Like the Soviet M1891/30 sniping rifle it had a turned-down bolt handle, but of a different form. This had a slot in it which could be used to tighten to mount which would hold its zero when removed. The vz.54 was replaced by the Dragunov SVD rifle in the 1970s. A small number were used in the Vietnam War.

The world's longest-lived military cartridge

If the Mosin-Nagant rifle was long-lived then the 7.62×54mmR cartridge was even more so, still being in production 125 years after its introduction in 1891. Again, there was nothing remarkable about its design as it looked backwards to the large-bore (11mm) black-powder, first-generation, centre-fire cartridges of the 1870s rather than anticipating those of the new century. Its resemblance to the 8×50mmR Lebel cartridge – little

Two views of the vz.54 sniping rifle. (NRA Museums, NRAMuseums.com)

more than the 11mm Gras cartridge of 1874 necked down to 8mm and given a load of smokeless propellant – is unremarkable given the degree of *détente* between Russia and France at the time. At first blush, its antiquated large, rimmed bottle-necked case was not conducive to its being adapted for automatic weapons. Yet its current survival is for use in a belt-fed machine gun and a self-loading rifle.

There were more modern cartridges available which the Russians could have copied or been influenced by. The 8mm Mauser cartridge of 1888 had a parallel-sided case with a semi-rim. It would be eventually developed into the 7.92×57mm Mauser cartridge and the legendary .30-06, and was the direct ancestor of the 7.62×51mm NATO round. As well as military derivatives, it spawned numerous commercial cartridges including the .270 and .243 Winchester.

The 7.62×54mmR was a dead-end cartridge that was obsolescent as soon as it was introduced. Even so, it has been in constant military production for 125 years and weapons chambered for it are still in service. The name of Colonel Nikolai Rogovtsev is often associated with the design of the 7.62×54mmR cartridge. Nothing is known of this officer, however, who was in all probability a Russian small-arms designer who worked closely with Sergei Mosin as the latter's rifle developed. The earliest cartridges had round-nosed, 211-grain (13.67g) cupronickel bullets and rounded cartridge bases which were supported by the dished face of the rifle's bolt head. In 1908, a lighter, 149-grain (9.65g) 'spitzer' bullet (the Type L) was introduced. This gave a much higher muzzle velocity (870m/sec as opposed to 620m/sec) and a flatter trajectory. The Type L bullet was found to be too light for use in machine guns, however, and in 1930 the Type D bullet was introduced to give better ranging characteristics. The Type D weighed 182 grains (11.79g) and developed a velocity of 810m/sec; it was identified by having a yellow tip. After the Great Patriotic War, the Type L and Type D bullets were phased out to be replaced by the LPS. This weighed 148 grains (9.59g), had a steel core and (sometimes) a white tip. The rounded profile of the cartridge head was changed, probably in 1930, to a more angular, bevelled form.

73

Assorted 7.62×54mmR Russian cartridges, including various ammunition natures with brass, copper-washed and lacquered-steel cases. Most have pointed 'spitzer' bullets but two have the original round-nosed M1891 bullets, while one is an early armour-piercing bullet. The cartridge at far left is loaded with a hunting bullet with an exposed lead tip. (Author's Collection)

The 7.62×54mmR cartridge was also loaded with a copper-tipped armour-piercing bullet during World War I. No tracer cartridge appears to have been issued until 1930, namely the Type T or T46. In 1932, the Soviet Union adopted an armour-piercing incendiary cartridge known as the B32. Short-range practice cartridges are known to have been developed, as were blank and dummy rounds with fluted cases and soldered bullet envelopes. The blanks have wooden or paper bullets and six-petal crimp closures. The early dummy cartridges resembled French examples with wooden bodies and false bullets. An explosive bullet was issued during 1915–16.

During World War I, millions of cartridges were loaded for Russia in the United States by Winchester Western and the Remington Union Metallic Cartridge Company. They were also loaded in the United Kingdom by Kynoch, Kings Norton Metal Company and Greenwood & Batley, and at various government cartridge factories. Those loaded by Kynoch have the company's name in Cyrillic letters as a headstamp: КАЙНОКВ.

Cartridges intended for use with the Soviet ShKAS aircraft machine gun (introduced in about 1934) had to be especially robust as the gun had a violent action, including a fast-rotating ten-shot feed cage. Cartridges suitable for the ShKAS gun bear the Cyrillic character Щ for 'Tsch' in their headstamps. It is unwise to fire these cartridges in rifles as they may develop excessive pressures.

During the Great Patriotic War, green- or grey-lacquered-steel cases were used as a way to save scarce cuprous metal. During the Cold War, steel cases washed in copper were used. Primers and case necks were often finished with green or red sealant for waterproofing purposes, but not as a means of indicating the nature of the ammunition. Although many countries loaded the 7.62×54mmR cartridge, there were few manufacturing deviations and a remarkable degree of consistency was achieved.

Today, the 7.62×54mmR cartridge is found loaded with five different forms of projectile, for use in sniping rifles and company-level machine guns. The 57-N-323S is a conventional steel-cored ball cartridge with a 148g bullet developing 830m/sec. The 7N13 is an armour-piercing bullet designed to defeat body armour; it has a 145g bullet developing 820m/sec. The green-tipped 7T2 tracer is a 149g bullet developing 800m/sec; tracer burn is 3 seconds. The black- and red-tipped 7BZ3 is an armour-piercing incendiary weighing 160g and developing 810m/sec. Finally, the 7N1 is an enhanced-accuracy sniper's bullet, weighing 151g and developing 820m/sec.

Beyond Russia and the Soviet Union, the following countries have loaded 7.62×54mmR ammunition during its 125-year currency: the People's Republic of China, Czechoslovakia, Egypt, Finland, France, East Germany, Hungary, Poland, Spain, Syria, the United Kingdom, the United States and Yugoslavia.

MOSIN-NAGANT CHARGERS

A charger containing five cartridges was developed in 1891 to allow the Russian soldier to fill the magazine of his rifle in one go. It was made of thin spring steel and had two integral springs cut into both ends of each side. The springs gripped the first and last cartridges in the charger and ensured that they did not fall out. In 1930, when the Mosin-Nagant rifle was modernized, the Soviets did away with the springs and simply folded the tip of the tops of the charger inwards to retain the cartridges. It is interesting to note that when the United Kingdom adopted chargers for its Lee-Enfield rifles in 1905, they bore a striking resemblance to the Russian M1891 charger. The British charger is made from heavier metal, however, and is much more robust; it saves on material by incorporating cut-outs in its design.

The People's Republic of China put up its cartridges in brass changers. There are modern-day Chinese copies of original M1891 chargers available via internet auction sites, but these copies are not very effective.

As originally issued, cartridges in chargers were put up in packets of 15 cartridges. The tops were secured by strings. After the Great Patriotic War, cartridges were supplied in 440-round 'sardine' cans, two of which came in a crate with a can-opener tool. The can lid provides a great deal of information including ammunition nature, manufacturer, batch, powder type and year of production. The cartridges in the cans were packed in paper wrappers, each wrapper containing 20 cartridges.

Most Russian-made chargers were stamped with a small arsenal mark. Those made during World War I by the Western Cartridge Company of East Altin, Illinois were distinguished by having two small holes in their bases. The holes were probably intended to enable US Ordnance personnel to inspect primers without having to remove the cartridges from the charger.

Russian

Early Izhevsk Arsenal	Small bow and arrow
Later Izhevsk Arsenal	Arrow in a triangle
Tula Arsenal	Small hammer

United States

Remington	1L R 17 (Mark 1 Land Service, Remington, 1917)
Western Cartridge Company	Unmarked; two small holes in base

United Kingdom

Greenwood & Batley	GB 1 1917
Hinks & Wells	1 Hinks Wells & Co 1917
Kynoch	ḰAЙHOKB 17
Myers & Son	MS 1917
Perry & Co	1/L P /17

Finland

G.W. Sohlberg Ab Oy	GWS
Tikkakoski	T in a triangle

Germany/Austria (World War I)

Deutsche Waffen- und Munitionsfabriken	DM in an oval
Austrian	W
Polte Magdeburg	PM in an oval

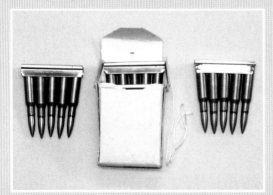

ABOVE 7.62×54mmR Russian cartridges in chargers. L to R: five cartridges in an M1891/30 charger (note lack of retaining springs to ends); original Soviet cardboard box with string closure, containing three chargers of five cartridges; five cartridges in an M1891 charger (note retaining springs at ends). (Author's Collection)

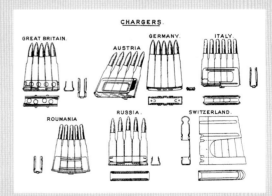

ABOVE Clips and chargers of seven countries as illustrated in the UK Government's 1929 publication *Textbook of Smallarms*. The similarity in cross-section between the Russian Mosin-Nagant charger and that of the British .303in Short Magazine Lee-Enfield (SMLE) bolt-action rifle is readily apparent. (Author's Collection)

CONCLUSION

Moscow, 7 November 2011:
Russian soldiers in World War II-
era Soviet military uniforms and
carrying Mosin-Nagant rifles of
the period participate in a military
parade to mark the 70th
anniversary of the 1941 parade,
when Red Army troops marched
past the Kremlin en route to the
front line to fight the invaders at
the gates of the Soviet capital.
(ALEXANDER NEMENOV/AFP/
Getty Images)

When the Russian Empire adopted the Mosin-Nagant rifle in 1891, it did so not because of the weapon's technological excellence but out of a sense of pan-Slavic national pride. For some time Russia had been reliant on foreign designers and manufacturers for her small arms. Here, at last, was a modern rifle that was designed (largely) by a Russian. However, the Russian manufacturing base was incapable of supplying the vast numbers of rifles needed to arm the Imperial Army. Once again Russia found itself dependent on foreign manufacturers.

The Mosin-Nagant M1891 rifle should have brought Russia into the modern military age with a small-bore, smokeless repeating rifle. To a

A Syrian fighter armed with an M1891/30 sniping rifle takes aim from a fortified position near Aleppo, 11 September 2014. The AK-47 assault rifle slung on the man's back would be useless for long-range, deliberate shots, hence the employment of this World War II-era M1891/30 for sniping. (BARAA AL-HALABI/AFP/Getty Images)

degree it did – at first – but events moved on, and the chaotic Russian military system was too bureaucratic to keep pace. In technological terms, the Mosin-Nagant is unique in that it has an interrupter plate in its receiver to prevent double loading in the magazine. That feature appears to have been largely redundant, however, making little (if any) contribution to the rifle's overall functionality. The Mosin-Nagant should have been modernized before World War I rather than in 1930. The Soviet modernization of the rifle did not go far enough and failed to produce the 'universal rifle' that was emerging elsewhere at the time. Only the Finnish models adopted in the late 1920s achieved any significant degree of modernization.

Ironically, due to a poor showing by Russia in World War I, the M1891 became a major asset for Russia's enemies, who captured vast quantities of rifles and ammunition. This in turn stimulated US arms production and meant that America became the world's arsenal once again. The mass deployment of the M1891/30 as a sniping rifle during the urban fighting of the Great Patriotic War would enable the Soviet Union to make a significant contribution to the defeat of German fascism; it allowed Soviet troops to dominate ground, destroy the German command structure and sap enemy morale.

The Mosin-Nagant served the Russian soldier and his Soviet successor as their principal firearm for some 60 years. It may have been crude by Western standards, but it was simple, reliable and robust, making it one of the most important military firearms ever issued. Ultimately, the Mosin-Nagant's true importance lies not in the design of the rifle, but in its cartridge, which remains the world's longest-serving military round.

BIBLIOGRAPHY

While the following list includes specific sources referred to during the writing of this book, more general histories of battles and campaigns often assist by allowing a greater perspective and context to be formed by the reader. It is generally beneficial to read about the scenarios in which the Mosin-Nagant rifle was used in order to get some idea of the tactical and practical limitations imposed on those who used it.

Archer, Denis H.R., ed. (1975). *Jane's Infantry Weapons 1976*, 2nd Edition. London: Jane's Yearbooks.

Barry, Quintin (2012). *War in the East: A Military History of the Russo-Turkish War 1877–78*. London: Helion.

Bekesi, Laszlo (2000). *Soviet Uniforms and Militaria 1917–1991*. Marlborough: Crowood Press.

Bekesi, Laszlo (2006). *Stalin's War – Soviet Uniforms and Militaria 1941–1945*. Marlborough: Crowood Press.

Bierman, Harris, R. (1972). 'The Finnish Mosin-Nagant Rifle', in Tanner, Hans, ed., *Guns of the World*. Los Angeles, CA: Petersen Publishing: pp. 280–85.

Black, Douglas (1989). 'The Guns of the German Navy 1914–1918', in Schroeder, Joseph J., ed., *Gun Collector's Digest*, 5th Edition. Northwood, IL: DBI Books.

Bogdanovic, Branko & Valencak, Ivan (1986). *Great Century of Guns*. New York, NY: Gallery Books.

Bradley, Joseph (1990). *Guns for the Tsar*. DeKalb, IL: Northern Illinois University Press.

Bradley, Ken (1994). *International Brigades in Spain 1936–39*. Elite 53. London: Osprey.

Brown, Leigh (2015). 'The Mosin Nagant – Russian Simplicity is Born', in *The Journal of the Historical Breechloading Smallarms Association*, Vol. 4, No. 7: 2–6.

Buttar, Prit (2014). *Collision of Empires: The War on the Eastern Front in 1914*. Oxford: Osprey.

Canfield, Bruce N. (2010). *U.S. Military Bolt Action Rifles*. Woonsocket, RI: Mowbray Publishing.

Carrick, Mike (2015). 'Winchester Model 1895: The WW1 Russian Contract', in *The Journal of the Historical Breechloading Smallarms Association*, Vol. 4, No. 7: 7–12.

Cornish, Nik (2001). *The Russian Army 1914–1918*. Men at Arms 364. Oxford: Osprey Publishing.

Craig, William (2015). *Enemy at the Gates: The Battle for Stalingrad*. New York, NY: Open Road Media. Originally published 1973.

Cudahy, John (1924). *Archangel: The American war with Russia, by a chronicler*. Chicago, IL: A.C. McClurg & Co.

Eby, Cecil (2007). *Comrades and Commissars: The Lincoln Battalion in the Spanish Civil War*. University Park, PA: Penn State University Press.

Finze, Wolfgang & Gortz, Joachim (2002). *Fremden Gewehre in deutschen Diensten 1914–1918*. Munich: self-published.

Forczyk, Robert (2015). *German Infantryman vs Russian Infantryman: 1914–1915*. Combat 11. Oxford: Osprey Publishing.

Gebhardt, Major James F. (2000). *The Official Soviet Mosin-Nagant Rifle Manual*. Boulder, CO: Paladin Press.

Hatch, Alden (1972). *Remington Arms in American History*. Bridgeport, CT: Remington Arms Co.

Herrick, William (no date). 'American writer William Herrick's account of his experiences as a volunteer in the Lincoln Battalion of the XVth International Brigade during the Spanish Civil War'. Available online at http://www.christiebooks.com/ChristieBooksWP/?s=herrick& searchsubmit= (accessed 11 May 2016).

Ivanov, Aleksei & Jowett, Philip (2004). *The Russo-Japanese War 1904–05*. Men at Arms 414. Oxford: Osprey Publishing.

Kuropatkin, General A.N., ed. Major E.D. Winton and trans. Captain A.B. Lindsay (1909). *The Russian Army and the Japanese War*. Vol. 1. New York, NY: E.P. Dutton & Co.

Labbet, P. (1980). *Military Small Arms Ammunition of the World 1945–1980*. London: Arms & Armour Press.

Labbet P. & Brown, F.A. (1994). *Foreign Rifle-Calibre Ammunition Manufactured in Britain*. Technical Ammunition Guide 1/6. London: self-published.

Labbet P. & Mead, P.J.F. (1987). *The 7.62mm×54 Cartridge – Imperial Russian and Communist*. Technical Ammunition Guide 3/1. London: self-published.

Lapin, Terence W. (2003). *The Mosin-Nagant Rifle*. 6th Edition. Tustin, CA: North Cape Publications.

McClintock, Major W (1889). *Foreign Attempts at Making Rifles of Smaller Calibre*. Technical Publications No. 196. Doncaster: D.P. & G. Military Publishers.

Mercaldo, Luke, et al. (2011). *Allied Rifle Contracts in America*. Greensboro, NC: Wet Dog Publications.

Merridale, Catherine (2005). *Ivan's War: The Red Army 1939–45*. London: Faber & Faber.

Mowbray, Stuart C. & Pulelo, J. (2009). *Bolt Action Military Rifles of the World*. Woonsocket, RI: Mowbray Publishing.

O'Riordan, Michael (2009). Interview with Erik Petersen. Available online at www.indymedia.ie (accessed 11 May 2016).

Orwell, George (1938). *Homage to Catalonia*. London: Secker & Warburg.

Pegler, Martin (2004). *Out of Nowhere: A History of the Military Sniper*. Oxford: Osprey Publishing.

Pegler, Martin (2015). *Winchester Lever-Action Rifles*. Weapon 42. Oxford: Osprey Publishing.

Priest, Graham (1993 & 1994). 'Trehlinejnaja Vintovka Obrasca 1891 Goda Bayonets', in *Guns Review* December 1993 (938–43), January 1994 (70–73) and February 1994 (111–14).

Schroeder, Joseph, ed. (1953). *Bannerman Catalogue of Military Goods - 1927*. Facsimile edition. Northfield, IL: DBI Books, Inc.

Sisemore, Major James D. (2003). *The Russo-Japanese War: Lessons Not Learned*. Available online at http://cgsc.cdmhost.com/cdm/singleitem/collection/p4013coll2/id/113 (accessed 26 February 2016).

Smith, Joseph E. (1973). *Small Arms of the World*. 10th Edition. New York, NY: Stackpole Books.

War Office (1929). *Textbook of Small Arms 1929*. London: HMSO.

Ward, Colonel John (1920). *With the 'Die-Hards' in Siberia*. London: Cassell & Co.

Warner, Denis & Warner, Peggy (2002). *The Tide at Sunrise: A History of the Russo-Japanese War, 1904–1905*. Abingdon: Frank Cass. Originally published in 1974 by Charterhouse Publishers, New York, NY.

Watts, John & White, Peter (1975). *The Bayonet Book*. Birmingham: self-published.

Webster, Donald B. (1993). *Bolt Action Military Rifles 1841–1918*. New York, NY: Museum Restoration Service.

Wolff, David, et al., eds (2007). *The Russo-Japanese War in Perspective: World War Zero*. Vol. II. Leiden: Brill.

Wrobel, Karl-Heinz (1999). *Drei Linien – Die Mosin Nagant Gewehr*. Vol. 1. Blaufelden: DWJ Verlags.

Wrobel, Karl-Heinz (2003). *Drei Linien – Die Mosin Nagant Gewehr*. Vol. 2. Blaufelden: DWJ Verlags.

Zaitsev, Vassili (2009). *Notes of a Russian Sniper*. Barnsley: Frontline Books.

Zuber, Terence (2011). *The Real German War Plan 1904–14*. Stroud: The History Press.

INDEX